THIRD EDITION

Compendium of Client Protection Rules

AMERICAN BAR ASSOCIATION
Center for Professional Responsibility

Cover design by Elizabeth Kulak/ABA Design

Printed in the United States of America.

30 29 28 27 26 5 4 3 2 1

The following Client Protection Rules constitute policies of the American Bar Association as adopted by its House of Delegates on the following dates: the Model Rules for Clients' Security Funds were adopted by the House of Delegates on August 12, 1981, amended as the Model Rules for Lawyers' Funds for Client Protection on August 9, 1989, and amended on August 13, 2002, August 7, 2006, and February 9, 2026; the Model Rules for Trust Account Overdraft Notification on February 9, 1988; the Model Rules on Financial Recordkeeping on February 9, 1993, and amended as the Model Rules for Client Trust Account Records on August 9, 2010; the Model Rule for Random Audit of Lawyer Trust Accounts on August 11, 1993; the Model Rule for Payee Notification on August 13, 1991; the Model Rules for Fee Arbitration on February 6, 2012; the Model Rules for Mediation of Client-Lawyer Disputes on August 4, 1998; the Guidelines for the Adoption of a Definition of the Practice of Law on August 11, 2003; the Model Court Rule on Insurance Disclosure on August 10, 2004; and the Model Court Rule on Provision of Legal Services Following Determination of Major Disaster on February 12, 2007.

Contents

Model Rules for Client Trust Account Records

Model Rule for Random Audit of Lawyer Trust Accounts

Model Rule for Payee Notification

Model Rules for Fee Arbitration

Model Rules for Mediation of Client—Lawyer Disputes

Guidelines for the Adoption of a Definition of the Practice of Law

Model Court Rule on Insurance Disclosure

Model Court Rule on Provision of Legal Services Following the Determination of Major Disaster

PREFACE

This volume is a compilation of policies adopted by the American Bar Association for the protection of the profession's clients and the public. The Model Rules were formulated by the Standing Committee on Public Protection in the Provision of Legal Services and the Guidelines by the Task Force on the Model Definition of the Practice of Law and then proposed to the ABA House of Delegates for adoption. The effort to develop these policies is based upon several premises:

- the practice of law is a profession;
- professionalism is a fundamental obligation of lawyers; and
- protection of client interests is at the heart of professionalism.

Nonetheless, noble intentions and aspirational goals are not enough. Measures taken to directly protect clients serve as a centerpiece of professionalism. In executing its mandate to enhance client protection, the Standing Committee has employed Model Rules as calls to action and found them effective.

Just as client protection is the centerpiece of professionalism, a viable lawyers' fund for client protection is the core of any client protection system. These funds arose in response to the bar's unwillingness to leave clients harmed by lawyer theft without a remedy. Thus, lawyers' fund awards are made by court-appointed trustees to replace money misappropriated within a client-lawyer relationship. All lawyers are besmirched by the wrongdoing of a few. But, all lawyers benefit if their fund takes care of the injured clients. This is the basis upon which lawyers financially support the fund, rather than relying on insurance to cover a shared risk. The assumption is that the vast majority of lawyers do not pose any risk whatever to Client Protection Funds, and that assumption is borne out by experience.

However few their numbers may be, dishonest lawyers can cause significant loss. Rather than simply reimbursing after the fact, jurisdictions sought mechanisms to limit losses, thus protecting the public without fund expenditures. The second rule presented, the *Model Rules for Trust Account Overdraft Notification*, is an excellent example. If a trust account check is returned for insufficient funds, one of two things has occurred: (a) either the lawyer or the bank has made a simple mistake, or (b) the lawyer is out-of-trust. Situation (a) can be readily demonstrated and easily forgotten, but situation (b) is as relevant a red flag to the system as can be imagined. The rule's concept is that disciplinary counsel receives a notice of dishonor simultaneously with notice to the bank's customers and the payees of the checks. There is very little burden to the bank, to the lawyer, or to disciplinary counsel, while the occasional early warning can be expected to save the system more money than the program costs.

Lawyers do not always understand the special requirements of trust accounting and financial recordkeeping inherent in a sound practice of law. *The Model Rules for Client Trust Account Records* are intended to help in this regard. Lawyers deserve an opportunity to know what is expected; they should not have to look beyond the rule for the fundamental principles. Lawyers can only benefit if such a rule is supplemented by courses in law school and continuing legal education programs, with sample sets of books and practical manuals made available as well.

How can the system ensure that lawyers understand the requirements of client trust account recordkeeping and are engaging in sound trust accounting practice? One way is with the *Model Rules for Random Audit of Lawyer Trust Accounts*. While most random audits conclude as purely educational, occasionally a lawyer who actively misappropriates from a trust account is discovered. Then, the random audit ceases and a disciplinary investigation ensues. In every other situation, no confusion should be permitted between random audits and audits for cause. Selection for the random audit program should be, as stated, purely random. No stigma whatever should attach to selection for audit.

When a third-party liability claim is settled, the client/claimant should not be the last to know. This is the basis for the *Model Rule for Payee Notification*, which is usually enacted either as an insurance regulation or a statute. It requires carriers to notify clients when payments of settlements are made to clients' lawyers or other representatives. The notice should be brief, plain and inexpensive to produce.

Notions of client protection extend beyond preventing and addressing misappropriation of client funds. The *Model Rules for Fee Arbitration and Model Rules for Mediation of Client-Lawyer Disputes* seek to provide fair, fast and inexpensive resolution of disputes involving legal fees and instances of alleged lesser misconduct. Since dissatisfaction with legal fees is consistently one of the highest causes of complaints registered against lawyers (along with the oft-related "failure to communicate"), avoidance of rancorous litigation is in everyone's best interests.

The *Guidelines for the Adoption of a Definition of the Practice of Law* address the fact that there are an increasing number of situations where members of the public, or lawyers licensed in a different state or territory, are providing services that are difficult to categorize under current statutes and case law as being, or not being, the delivery of legal services. The adoption by states and territories of a definition of the practice of law is an important step in protecting the public from unqualified service providers and in eliminating uncertainty for persons working in law-related areas, including lawyers licensed in other states or territories, about the propriety of their conduct.

The *Model Court Rule on Insurance Disclosure* requires lawyers to disclose on their annual registration statements whether they maintain professional liability insurance. The Model Court Rule allows potential clients to make fully informed decisions whether to hire particular lawyers by allowing those potential clients access to relevant information related to the lawyers' representation. The information submitted by lawyers will be made available by such means as designated by the highest court in the jurisdiction.

The *Model Court Rule on Provision of Legal Services Following Determination of Major Disaster* addresses the provision of pro bono legal services by out-of-state lawyers in a jurisdiction that has been devastated by a major disaster. It also addresses the issue of whether lawyers whose practices have been disrupted by a major disaster can continue their law practices on a temporary basis in a jurisdiction in which they are not otherwise authorized to practice law.

This last point applies to all these programs. Client protection measures worthy of the name are not anti-lawyer; they protect the profession as well as clients. Client protection is where altruism and prudence meet for the legal profession. The programs presented in these Model Rules and Guidelines can be implemented without vast expenditure of resources and are worthy of consideration by bar leaders in all jurisdictions. While these Model Rules and Guidelines have aspirational aspects, they are not "pie in the sky" concepts. Rather, they reflect actual programs successfully administered in a number of jurisdictions, some for many years.

Just because Model Rules and Guidelines are available does not mean that they cannot be improved. Indeed, one of the benefits of availability is that suggested improvements might be forthcoming. Programs, as enacted, necessarily feature variations owing to local custom, culture and law. It is hoped that new ideas that work well will be shared.

Any Prefaces that precede, and the Comments that follow, the Model Rules or Guidelines have not been adopted by the ABA House of Delegates and, therefore, do not reflect the policy of the American Bar Association. The Comments are offered as explanatory information to assist in the interpretation of the Rules and Guidelines and to provide guidance for implementing client protection programs. Text in brackets ("[ ]") denotes an alternative or suggested discretionary provision of the Model Rule.

Daniel J. Crothers[1]

1. Daniel J. Crothers is a former Chair of the ABA Standing Committee on Client Protection and the ABA Standing Committee on Professional Regulation.

A HISTORY OF THE CLIENT PROTECTION RULES

Remedies for defalcation of clients' funds by lawyers were established in English Commonwealth countries at the beginning of the 20th century.[1] Developments in the law regarding lawyers' responsibilities appear to be tied historically to depressed economic times during which lawyers misappropriated client funds.

The first major development in the protection of client funds arose in the turmoil of the Boer War (1899–1902) when the English stock market tumbled, sending many solicitors and well established firms into bankruptcy. Until then, solicitors commonly commingled their own funds with client funds and even used clients' funds, unless earmarked for a particular purpose.[2]

The severe losses following the market collapse prompted Parliament in 1901 to amend the Larceny Act of 1861[3] to make it a criminal offense to convert funds or property held in trust. The expansion of criminal liability for defalcation was not accompanied by passage of civil laws requiring the segregation of client funds; by 1907, however, solicitor's training included bookkeeping courses.

The English Law Society established a special committee to examine professional accounting requirements and the possible formation of a Guarantee Fund to protect defrauded clients. The special committee concluded that solicitors were duty bound to make a full and proper accounting of clients' funds by maintaining separate accounts. Further protections were considered unnecessary.[4] It was not until Parliamentary amendments

1. This overview does not include the development of client protection mechanisms throughout the world, but focuses on developments in the English Commonwealth countries that provided the matrix for client protection funds in the United States in the 20th century.

2. Kenneth Jarvis, Lecture, Negligence and Fraud C Symptoms of Malaise 2, Meredith Memorial Lectures, Faculty of Law McGill University (1984) [hereinafter Jarvis] (on file at ABA Center for Professional Responsibility). Barristers were not originally and are not currently subject to such rules, because only solicitors, but not barristers, accept client funds to hold in trust. This is a common distinction in all English Commonwealth countries.

3. Larceny Acts, 1861 to 1901, 1 Edw. 7, ch. 10 (amendment 1901).

4. Jarvis, *supra* note 2, at 2.

were made to the Solicitors' Act, 1933,[5] that the Law Society was required to draft rules requiring solicitors to establish segregated client accounts and to maintain records of those accounts.

While the English Law Society declined to recommend the creation of a compensation fund in 1907,[6] New Zealand emerged as a leader in the development of client protection remedies, particularly with the passage in 1908[7] of a provision requiring solicitors to deposit client funds into bank trust accounts. This was followed in 1913 with amendments empowering the New Zealand Law Society to make rules requiring audits of solicitors' trust accounts.[8]

Despite these provisions, losses by defaulting solicitors came to the attention of the New Zealand Parliament in 1926, and the Attorney General, who recommended that the New Zealand Law Society draft and introduce legislation regarding solicitors' accounting of client trust funds. The Association of New Zealand Chambers of Commerce presented a resolution in February 1927, providing:

> [t]hat this Conference brings before the Law Society the necessity of Solicitors handling trust moneys, subscribing to an adequate indemnity insurance, or failing that, the Law Society provides a guarantee fund to admitted solicitors similar to the guarantee funds provided by the banks.[9]

That March, the concerns of Parliament and the Association of Chambers of Commerce were re viewed by the New Zealand Law Society Council when the Council of the Wellington District Law Society proposed the "creation of a fund for the purpose of making provision for monetary losses incurred by clients of defaulting solicitors."[10] The measure prompted the formation of a committee to study legislation regarding Solicitors' Trust Accounts and to work with the New Zealand Attorney General in the formulation of legislation. After prolonged discussions the Law Society

5. The Solicitors' Act, 1933, 23 & 24 Geo. 5, ch. 24 (1). The Law Society adopted The Solicitors' Account Rules in 1935.

6. Jarvis, *supra* note 2, at 2.

7. Law Practitioners' Act, 1908, 7 Edw. 7, No. 100, § 47.

8. Law Practitioners' Act, 1913, 4 Geo. 5, No. 72, § 14.

9. Minutes of the Council of the New Zealand Law Society, March 25, 1927.

10. *Id.*

drafted a bill that was passed by the New Zealand Parliament creating the first trust fund, the Solicitors' Fidelity Guarantee Fund.[11]

When originally established, the fund reimbursed those who suffered monetary losses because of theft by a solicitor or a solicitor's servant or agent of any money or other valuable property entrusted to the solicitor in the course of practice. All solicitors were required to contribute to the fund. After the Act was adopted, the Law Society drafted an advertising circular, for publication by local law societies, informing the public about the fund benefits.

In 1930, the Legal Practitioners' Fidelity Guarantee Fund was established in Queensland, Australia.[12] The first fidelity fund in Canada was established in Alberta in 1939, and entitled the Assurance Fund.[13] A compensation fund was created in England in 1941 into which every practicing solicitor was required to contribute annually.[14] Funds were established in Scotland in 1949[15] and Ireland in 1954.[16]

World War II may have played a prominent, if unexpected, role in the development of lawyers' funds for client protection in the United States. According to one history of the development of such funds, Kenneth G. McGilvray, of Sacramento, California, learned about the fund concept while stationed in New Zealand during the war and returned home to publish an article discussing the New Zealand experience in the California State Bar Journal in 1946.[17]

Several years later, in 1953, Robert G. Storey, then American Bar Association (ABA) president, discussed lawyers' funds for client protection in his report to the Association. Interest in the funds was stimulated by New Jersey Supreme Court Chief Justice Arthur G. Vanderbilt and Harvard Law School Dean Erwin Griswold. The ABA established a committee in 1955 to study and promote the creation of such funds.[18]

---

11. The Law Practitioner's Amendment (Solicitors' Fidelity Guarantee Fund) Act, 1929, 20 Geo. 5, No. 15. These provisions were then included in a consolidation of various measures regarding solicitors in the Law Practitioners' Act, 1931, 22 Geo. 5, No. 46.

12. The Queensland Law Society Act of 1952, 1 Eliz. 2, No. 24, § 9(2)(F).

13. Legal Profession Act, § 31a, amending the Legal Profession Act (Alberta, Canada 1939).

14. The Solicitors Act, 1941, Geo. 6, ch. 46 §§ 2, 4 &. 5

15. The Legal Aid and Solicitors' (Scotland) Act, 1949, 12 & 13 Geo. 6. ch. 63, § 22.

16. Solicitors Act, 1954, Acts of the Oireachtais, No. 36, § 69.

17. ABA, Report on Clients' Security Funds 5 (1964) (Report issued by the Junior Bar Conference).

18. *Id.*

In the United States, 1959 stands out as a watershed year in the development of client protection measures. The first American lawyers' fund for client protection was established in Vermont in January 1959 through the auspices of the Vermont Bar Association. In February, the ABA House of Delegates adopted a resolution approving such funds in principle and urging all state bar associations to appoint feasibility study committees. In May, the Board of Governors of the Illinois State Bar Association adopted a resolution approving the principle of a fund and appointing a committee to develop ways to establish a fund with the Chicago Bar Association. In June, the Philadelphia Bar Association adopted a resolution putting a clients' security fund into operation. In August, a meeting of the ABA Clients' Security Fund Committee reported that 34 state bar associations had appointed committees to study fund creation. In September the State Bar of Washington voted to establish a security fund. The next month, bar associations in Colorado and New Mexico followed suit. In November the Board of Governors of the Virginia State Bar Association approved the establishment of a fund in principle.[19] By 1976, 47 jurisdictions had established some form of lawyers' funds for client protection.[20] By 1998, all jurisdictions in the United States and Canada had established a fund. The organization, funding, accessibility and responsiveness to client claims vary widely among the funds.

Model Rules for Lawyers' Funds for Client Protection

Since 1969 the ABA Standing Committee on Public Protection in the Provision of Legal Services (PPPLS) formerly known as the Committee on Client Protection has actively promoted the establishment, maintenance and improvement of lawyers' funds for client protection for the benefit of the public and the profession. The Committee published *Suggested Guidelines for the Establishment and Operation of a Clients' Security Fund* in the mid-1970s, and in 1979 began its effort to codify into black-letter the basic mechanism to achieve reimbursement of losses generated by the dishonest conduct of lawyers.

19. Robert Gigi, *Pennsylvania Clients' Security Fund—How Secure is the Public?*, 22 Vill. L. Rev. 452, 455 (1977).

20. Rev. 452, 455 (1977).

In 1981, the ABA House of Delegates approved the *Model Rules for Clients' Security Funds*. Nearly a decade later, based on experience in reimbursement programs nationally, the rules were updated and renamed *Model Rules for Lawyers' Funds for Client Protection*. The revisions were adopted by the ABA House of Delegates in 1989.

Over the ensuing years other important safeguards have been developed by the various jurisdictions that have led to the development of other important Model Rules by the Standing Committee on Public Protection. (The Standing Committee on Lawyers' Responsibility for Client Protection was constituted in 1984 through a merger of the Standing Committee on Clients' Security Fund and the Standing Committee on the Unauthorized Practice of Law. In 1997 the Committee was renamed the Standing Committee on Client Protection. Finally, in 2018, the Committee was renamed the Standing Committee on Public Protection in the Provision of Legal Services, also known as the PPPLS Committee, to better reflect its mission to protect the public interest, at large rather than just clients.)

In August 2002, the ABA House of Delegates accepted a package of revisions to the *Model Rules for Lawyers' Funds for Client Protection*. Additional revisions were made in 2011 and 2026. The amendments reflect experience gained during the four decades that have elapsed since the original Model Rules were adopted. Every U.S. jurisdiction now has a fund to compensate clients for financial loss resulting from their lawyer's dishonesty. Rather than making significant changes, the revisions are intended to fine-tune aspects of lawyers' funds for client protection.

Model Rules for Trust Account Overdraft Notification

Lawyers are required to maintain client funds in specially designated escrow or trust accounts, according to Rule 1.15 of the ABA *Model Rules of Professional Conduct*. In 1988, the ABA House of Delegates adopted the *Model Rules for Trust Account Overdraft Notification*, requiring financial institutions to notify the state lawyer disciplinary agency when an overdraft has occurred in a lawyers' trust or escrow account. This rule is designed to operate as an "early warning" that a lawyer may be engaging in conduct that might injure clients.

Model Rule for Payee Notification

In 1991, the ABA House of Delegates approved a *Model Rule for Payee Notification* that requires insurers to provide written notice to a claimant that payment was delivered to the claimant's lawyer or other representative by draft, check or otherwise. This Model Rule was based on Regulation 64 of the Department of Insurance of the State of New York, 11 NYCRR 216.9, promulgated in 1988, that had proved highly successful in protecting client interests.

Model Rules for Client Trust Account Records

The *Model Rules for Client Trust Account Records* were adopted by the ABA House of Delegates in August 2010 to replace the *Model Rule on Financial Recordkeeping*. The *Model Rules for Client Trust Account Records* delineates the types of records a lawyer must maintain to satisfy the requirements of Rule 1.15 of the *Model Rules of Professional Conduct* that a lawyer must preserve "complete records" with respect to trust accounts and render a "full accounting" for the receipt and distribution of trust account property.

Model Rule for Random Audit of Lawyer Trust Accounts

The *Model Rule for Random Audit of Trust Accounts* was approved in August 1993. Adoption of such a rule had been included as Recommendation Number 16 in the Report of the Commission on the Evaluation of Disciplinary Enforcement, otherwise known as the "McKay Commission," which the ABA House of Delegates adopted in February 1992.

The McKay Commission had found by 1992 that trust account notification, recordkeeping and random audit rules had been adopted by a sufficient number of jurisdictions so that a body of experience was able to demonstrate that these programs were effective deterrents as well as detectors of thefts of funds by lawyers. Consequently, the Commission recommended the highest court in each jurisdiction adopt a rule authorizing the lawyer disciplinary agency to conduct audits of lawyer trust accounts selected at random without having a basis to believe misconduct occurred.

When this Model Rule was adopted, random audit programs existed in Delaware, Iowa, Nebraska, New Hampshire, New Jersey, New York (1st and 2d Departments), North Carolina and the state of Washington.

Model Rules for Fee Arbitration

Another important series of recommendations in the McKay Commission report centered around the establishment of procedures for handling the numerous complaints received by disciplinary agencies that do not involve allegations of lawyer misconduct, but reflect legitimate client concerns. Among these, the Commission recommended adoption of a program for the mandatory arbitration of fee disputes.

As a result of this recommendation, the ABA House of Delegates in February 1995 adopted the *Model Rules for Fee Arbitration*. These rules were based on experience in six states that had programs for mandatory fee arbitration: Alaska, California, Maine, New Jersey, South Carolina and Wyoming. The rules were amended in February 2012 to reflect the evolution of Fee Arbitration programs to refine current practices in order to increase productivity, efficiency, and fairness.

Model Rules for Mediation of Client-Lawyer Disputes

On August 4, 1998, at its Annual meeting in Toronto, the ABA House of Delegates adopted the black-letter of the *Model Rules for Mediation of Client-Lawyer Disputes*. The mediation process will benefit the public by directly addressing instances where a lawyer is alleged to have engaged in lesser misconduct but the misconduct does not warrant a formal disciplinary proceeding. A mediation program will also protect the public by removing matters involving lesser misconduct from the disciplinary system and thereby allowing disciplinary counsel to focus their efforts on more serious matters.

Guidelines for the Adoption of a Definition of the Practice of Law

On August 11, 2003 the ABA House of Delegates adopted the Report and Recommendation of the Task Force on the Model Definition of the Practice of Law. The *Guidelines for the Adoption of a Definition of the Practice of Law* recommend that every jurisdiction and territory adopt a definition of the practice of law that includes the basic premise that the practice of law is the application of legal principles and judgment to the circumstances or objectives of another person or entity and that each state and territory should determine who may engage in the practice of law and under what circumstances, based upon the potential harm and benefit to the public. The determination should include consideration of minimum qualifications, competence and accountability.

There are an increasing number of situations where nonlawyers, or lawyers licensed in a different state or territory, are providing services that are difficult to categorize under current statutes and case law as being, or not being, the delivery of legal services. The adoption by jurisdictions and territories of a definition of the practice of law is an important step in protecting the public from unqualified service providers and in eliminating uncertainty for persons working in law-related areas, including lawyers licensed in other states or territories, about the propriety of their conduct.

Model Court Rule on Insurance Disclosure

On August 10, 2004, the ABA House of Delegates adopted the *Model Court Rule on Insurance Disclosure*. The Model Court Rule requires lawyers to disclose on their annual registration statements whether they maintain professional liability insurance. It places an affirmative duty upon lawyers to notify the highest court whenever the insurance policy covering the lawyer's conduct lapses or is terminated. This ensures that the information reported to the highest court is accurate during the entire reporting period. Lawyers who do not comply with the Model Court Rule are not unauthorized to practice law until they comply. The purpose of the Rule is to provide a potential client with access to relevant information related to a lawyer's representation in order to make an informed decision about whether to hire a particular lawyer.

The information submitted by lawyers will be made available by such means as designated by the highest court in the jurisdiction. For example, in Illinois, Kansas, Nebraska and Virginia, information regarding a lawyer's professional liability insurance is made available to a potential client if the client requests that information. The information can also be accessed on the bars' websites. (See, www.vsb.org, under the headings Public Information, Attorney Records Search, Attorneys without Malpractice Insurance).

Model Court Rule on Provision of Legal Services Following Determination of Major Disaster

On February 12, 2007, the ABA House of Delegates adopted the *Model Court Rule on Provision of Legal Services Following Determination of Major Disaster*. The Model Court Rule provides that, after the highest court in an affected jurisdiction, or in another jurisdiction to which displaced persons temporarily relocate, determines that an emergency exists that affects the state's justice system and the provision of legal services, the court may allow: (1) out-of-state lawyers to provide *pro bono* legal services to the citizens of the affected state within certain constraints described in the model rule; and (2) lawyers from an affected state can provide legal services in an unaffected state on a temporary basis if these services are reasonably related to the lawyer's practice in the affected jurisdiction. The Model Court Rule incorporates the fundamental and well settled Association policy that regulation of the legal profession vests with the judicial branch of government. The provision of temporary *pro bono* legal services under the Model Court Rule shall be assigned and supervised through an established not-for-profit bar association, *pro bono* program or legal services program or through such organization specifically designated by the highest court. The Model Court Rule requires out-of-state lawyers to file a registration statement with the Clerk of the Court in a form prescribed by the Court. Under paragraph (b) of the Model Court Rule, an *emeritus* lawyer from another United States jurisdiction may provide *pro bono* legal services on a temporary basis in an affected jurisdiction.

ABA MODEL RULES FOR LAWYERS' FUNDS FOR CLIENT PROTECTION

Adopted by the House of Delegates as the Model Rules for Clients' Security Funds on August 12, 1981, and amended, as the Model Rules for Lawyers' Funds for Client Protection, August 9, 1989 and amended on August 13, 2002, August 6, 2006, and February 9, 2026.

American Bar Association Standing Committee on Public Protection in the Provision of Legal Services 2025–2026

Lindsey D. Draper, *Chair*
Wauwatosa, Wisconsin

Gabriel Huertas
Albany, New York

Matthew Kaiser
Washington, District of Columbia

Ellen Murphy
Winston-Salem, North Carolina

Claire Reynolds
Austin, Texas

Timothy Samuelson
Madison, Wisconsin

Deborah Winokur
Philadelphia, Pennsylvania

David Weyant, *Special Advisor*
Calgary, Alberta, Canada

Beverly Carroll, *Liaison*
ABA Board of Governors
Rock Hill, South Carolina

Linda Bauer, *Liaison*
National Client Protection Organization
Boston, Massachusetts

Craig Bray, *Liaison*
National Organization of Bar Counsel
Seattle, Washington

Center for Professional Responsibility

Director
Jason Vail

Public Protection Counsel
Stephanie D. Custard

MODEL RULES FOR LAWYERS' FUNDS FOR CLIENT PROTECTION

PREFACE

The *Model Rules for Lawyers' Funds for Client Protection* are intended to serve as a national model for establishment and administration of a client protection fund. However, they cannot expect to accommodate every need of each Fund given the unique regulatory characteristics of each jurisdiction. The Model Rules aspire to establish standards for effective financing and efficient administration of Funds to achieve the purpose of client protection. They continue the basic intent and aspiration of the original Model Rules for Lawyers' Client Security Funds: to provide meaningful, prompt, and cost-free reimbursement to clients who have been injured by a lawyer's dishonest conduct.

Despite the best attempts of the legal profession to establish high standards of ethics and appropriate disciplinary sanctions for their breach, it is a fact that some lawyers misappropriate money from their clients. Typically, those lawyers lack the financial wherewithal to make restitution to their victims.

The organized bar throughout the United States has responded by creating Client Protection Funds to provide necessary reimbursement. Under a variety of names, the Funds were either created by court rule, legislation or by the voluntary action of bar associations. In jurisdictions in which the bar is mandatory (i.e, membership in the state bar association is required to have a license to practice law), the Fund may be part of the state bar association, which performs a variety of functions related to professional responsibility (e.g., administration of the lawyer regulatory system).

Resourcing a Fund can be generated from a variety of sources including mandatory assessment, legislative budget appropriation, and voluntary contribution. Mandatory assessment by court rule has proven to be the preferred method of assuring continual funding and staffing. Funds that receive revenues through mandatory assessment are preferred because the result is a reliable and predictable source of income. This allows a Fund to fully reimburse losses and to engage in public information, continuing legal education programs, and related activities. Voluntary contribution is the weakest funding method; it does not provide the Fund with broad-based and permanent income.

Rule 1. Purpose and Scope

A. The purpose of the Lawyers' Fund for Client Protection is to promote public confidence in the administration of justice and the integrity of the legal profession by reimbursing losses caused by the dishonest conduct of lawyers licensed or otherwise authorized to practice law in this jurisdiction occurring in the course of the client-lawyer or other fiduciary relationship between the lawyer and the claimant.

B. For purposes of these Rules, "lawyer" shall include a person:

(1) licensed to practice law in this jurisdiction, regardless of where the lawyer's conduct occurs;

(2) employed as in-house counsel;

(3) admitted *pro hac vice*;

(4) licensed and permitted to practice in this jurisdiction as a foreign legal consultant;

(5) admitted only in a non-United States jurisdiction but who is otherwise authorized to practice law in this jurisdiction; or

(6) recently suspended or disbarred whom clients reasonably believed to be licensed to practice law when the dishonest conduct occurred.

C. Every lawyer has an obligation to the public to participate in the collective effort of the bar to reimburse persons who have lost money or property as a result of the dishonest conduct of another lawyer. Contribution to the Lawyers' Fund for Client Protection is an acceptable method of meeting this obligation.

Comment

[1] Paragraph A expresses the general purpose of a Lawyers' Fund for Client Protection: promoting public confidence in the administration of justice and the integrity of the legal profession. The term "dishonest conduct" is defined in Rule 10.

[2] The definition of lawyer, found in Paragraph B, includes not only persons licensed or otherwise authorized to practice law in this jurisdiction, but also lawyers practicing law in this jurisdiction as inhouse counsel admission, through *pro hac vice* admission, as a licensed foreign legal consultant admission authorized to engage in the temporary practice of

law, and by former or suspended lawyers reasonably believed by clients to have been authorized to practice law at the time the dishonest conduct occurred. Lawyers employed as in-house counsel, *pro hac vice*, or as foreign legal consultants should both pay into the Fund as provided under Rule 3 and have their conduct covered by the Fund.

[3] The Fund is part of this jurisdiction's system of lawyer regulation. The Fund therefore has jurisdiction to recognize claims filed against lawyers licensed to practice law in this jurisdiction regardless of where the lawyer's conduct occurs. This is consistent with the jurisdictional authority set forth in Rule 8.5 (a) of the ABA *Model Rules of Professional Conduct*: "A lawyer admitted in this jurisdiction is subject to the disciplinary authority of this jurisdiction, regardless of where the lawyer's conduct occurs." Pursuant to Paragraph B, if necessary, this Fund is authorized to "follow" the lawyer and compensate eligible claimants who have suffered losses as a result of the lawyer's dishonest conduct.

[4] It is particularly equitable to require that this Fund, into which lawyers have paid annual assessments, have the primary responsibility to compensate clients who have suffered losses.

[5] Rule 10(E) provides for an equitable balancing test to determine whether the Fund, another jurisdiction's Fund, or both Funds should pay claims filed against lawyers not admitted or authorized to practice law exclusively in this jurisdiction.

[6] Paragraph C, drawn from the Comment to Rule 1.15 of the ABA *Model Rules of Professional Conduct*, recognizes that lawyers individually and the bar collectively, have the obligation to participate in a Lawyers' Fund for Client Protection.

Rule 2. Establishment

A. There is established the Lawyers' Fund for Client Protection ("Fund") to reimburse claimants for losses caused by dishonest conduct committed by lawyers admitted to practice in this state.

B. There is established, under the supervision of the highest court in this jurisdiction ("Court"), the Lawyers' Fund for Client Protection Board of Trustees ("Board"), which shall receive, hold, manage and disburse from the Fund such monies as may from to time be allocated to the Fund.

C. **Monies allocated to the Fund shall constitute a separate and inviolate independent trust fund.**

D. **These rules shall be effective for claims filed with the Board after [date] and the Board shall not pay claims for losses incurred as a result of dishonest conduct committed prior thereto.**

Comment

[1] The practice of law is so directly connected to the exercise of judicial power and the administration of justice that the right to define and regulate it belongs to the judicial department. It is the court that bears the responsibility for establishing qualifications for practice and for seeing that lawyers subject to its jurisdiction adhere to the standards of conduct the Court mandates.

[2] Paragraph B links the establishment of a Fund to the Court's power to regulate the practice of law. The Court has the inherent power to establish a Fund and require lawyers admitted to practice in this jurisdiction to contribute to it. The Court not only has the power but also the duty to provide a system for reimbursement to clients whose lawyers have mishandled their funds. The Court appointed Board of Trustees, or its equivalent, should be vested as fiduciaries with sole authority and independent discretion in the administration of the Fund and its assets.

[3] Paragraph C ensures that vital to the success of the Fund, assets allocated to its operation and payment of reimbursement claims must not be vulnerable to reallocation or use by other agencies or organizations or subject to capture by other branches of government.

[4] The limitation imposed in Paragraph D is necessary to prevent the possibility of an immediate bankrupting of the Fund caused by the payment of claims for dishonest conduct committed before the Fund was established. The provision sets a time certain after which losses will be reimbursable.

RULE 3. FUNDING

A. **The Court shall provide for funding by the lawyers admitted and licensed to practice law in the jurisdiction in amounts adequate for the proper payment of claims and the costs of administering the Fund.**

B. A lawyer's failure to pay any fee assessed shall be a cause for suspension from practice until payment has been made.

C. Monies collected for a Fund shall be deposited to a separate and inviolate independent public trust fund.

D. There shall be no reduction or suspension of funding as a result of a Fund carrying a surplus balance.

Comment

[1] Paragraph A suggests that the single most important factor in establishing and maintaining an effective client reimbursement program is ensuring adequate and continuous funding through a reliable source. The Court, pursuant to its authority to assess an annual fee to finance systems that implement the Court's regulatory authority.

[2] Paragraph B is the enforcement mechanism for the failure to pay the assessment. See Paragraph A of Rule 16 for restitution and subrogation enforcement standards.

[3] Paragraph D reflects the reality that it is not possible for a Fund to predict the exact annual cost of reimbursement awards, or when catastrophic claims may arise. Funds should not be penalized for carrying a positive balance or surplus funds; which serve to ensure their financial stability and ability to be responsive to client needs as they arise.

Rule 4. Fund

All monies or other assets of the Fund shall constitute an independent public trust and shall be held in the name of the Fund, subject to the direction of the Board.

Comment

[1] Under Rule 3, the fees assessed by the Court are to be used for a stated purpose, the Fund.

[2] Matters and expenses for which the Fund may be used should be considered and delineated by the Board in written policies to ensure that claimants receive the maximum benefit possible from available sources. Segregating any accounts in the name of the Fund is fundamental in preventing the use of monies by other entities for purposes unrelated to reimbursement and client protection.

[3] Administrative expenses will be incurred by operating a Fund even though trustees traditionally serve on the Board without compensation.

The cost of administering the Fund, e.g., expenses of Trustees, hearing of claims, recordkeeping, and salaries for staff and other overhead, should be paid out from the Fund.

RULE 5. COMPOSITION AND OFFICERS OF THE BOARD

A. The Board shall consist of five lawyers and two public members appointed by the Court for initial terms as follows:

(1) two lawyers for one year;

(2) one public member for two years;

(3) two lawyers for two years;

(4) one public member for three years; and

(5) one lawyer for three years.

Subsequent appointments shall be for a term of three years. The Court may limit the number of successive terms that Trustees may serve on the Board.

B. Trustees shall serve without compensation but shall be reimbursed for their actual and necessary expenses incurred in the discharge of their duties.

C. Vacancies shall be filled by appointment by the Court for any unexpired terms.

D. The Board shall select a Chair, Secretary, Treasurer and such other officers as the Board deems appropriate.

E. The Treasurer shall be bonded in such manner and amount as the Board shall determine.

Comment

[1] A Board composed of lawyers and public members results in balanced evaluation of claims within the full context of the client-lawyer relationship. Participation by public members enhances the credibility of the reimbursement process in the eyes of the public. Trustees should reflect all segments of the profession and the general population.

[2] A Board of seven members is small enough to accomplish the work of the Fund, yet not so large as to discourage active involvement by each member or to be cumbersome. Terms of office are staggered to encourage continuity of experience and the development of policy and precedent. Depending on local policy or experience, the Court may limit successive appointments of the Trustees.

[3] The Trustees should serve without compensation, *pro bono publico*, but should be reimbursed for expenses incurred in the discharge of their office.

[4] Since direct and full responsibility for the administration and management of the Fund and its assets is vested in the Board, it should select its own officers.

Rule 6. Board Meetings

A. The Board shall meet as frequently as necessary to conduct the business of the Fund and to timely process claims.

B. The Chair shall call a meeting at any reasonable time or upon the request of at least two Trustees.

C. A quorum for any meeting of the Board shall be four Trustees. A motion shall pass upon the affirmative vote of four Trustees.

D. Minutes of meeting shall be taken and permanently maintained by the Secretary.

Comment

[1] Regular and frequent meetings of the Board throughout the year are necessary to ensure that the Fund has the ability to respond promptly and effectively. The Board should meet at least quarterly if any claims are pending. Video conferencing should be encouraged where necessary to ensure that claims are handled in as expeditious a manner as possible consistent with their just resolution.

Rule 7. Duties and Responsibilities of the Board

The Board shall have the following duties and responsibilities:

A. to receive, evaluate, determine and pay claims;

B. to promulgate rules of procedure not inconsistent with these Rules;

C. to prudently invest such portions of the funds as may not be needed currently to pay losses, and to maintain sufficient reserves as appropriate;

D. to provide a full report at least annually to the Court and to make other reports as necessary or as the Court directs;

E. to publicize its activities to potential claimants, the public and the bar;

F. to employ adequate staff to assure the Board's effective and efficient performance of its functions;

G. to retain and compensate consultants, administrative staff, investigators, actuaries, agents, legal counsel and other persons as necessary;

H. to prosecute claims for restitution to which the Fund is entitled;

I. to engage in studies and programs for client protection and prevention of dishonest conduct by lawyers;

J. to promote effective communication between lawyer disciplinary authorities and the Fund;

K. to examine witnesses and, in accordance with [applicable state rules of civil procedure] and the rules and regulations of the trustees; administer oaths or affirmations and issue subpoenas; and

L. to perform all other acts necessary or proper for the fulfillment of the purposes and effective administration of the Fund.

Comment

[1] In determining the order and manner of payment of claims, the Board should have the discretion to pay in subsequent years all or part of claims that were not fully reimbursed in a prior year.

[2] Investing monies that are not needed to cover current claims permits a reasonable return without risking the integrity of the Fund. The Board should adopt specific guidelines for the investment of funds. Investments should be of appropriate duration to maintain liquidity of assets and enable the Board to promptly pay losses. The nature of the investments may be specifically limited to bonds, notes or securities issued or guaranteed by a state or federal agency, interest bearing accounts or certificates of deposit.

[3] Paragraphs D and E require public information programs. The Board has the affirmative obligation to publicize its activities to both bench and bar. Similarly it is incumbent on the Board to publicize itself to the general public. The fulfillment of both obligations is extremely important to the success of the Fund in achieving its purposes.

[4] As suggested in Paragraph I, the Board also should study and, if appropriate, adopt other potential programs, such as trust account

overdraft notification, payee notification, and random audits, to help reduce defalcation.

[5] The Fund's assets should not be unduly diminished by employing investigative or other personnel whose work would duplicate the efforts of others responsible for investigating lawyers' professional conduct. See Rule 12C regarding the cooperative effort anticipated between the Board and the lawyer disciplinary authority. Moreover, the Fund shall establish mechanisms to encourage the lawyer disciplinary authority to notify complainants about the existence of the Fund.

[6] The Board should make an attempt to prosecute all claims for restitution. Restitution is one way of replenishing the Fund's assets. See also, Rule 16 which focuses on subrogation and other methods of restitution.

[7] The Trustees and staff should also participate in seminars and continuing legal educational programs dealing with client protection.

Rule 8. Conflict of Interest

A. A Trustee who has or has had a client-lawyer relationship, a financial relationship, or a significant personal relationship with a claimant or lawyer who is the subject of a claim shall not participate in the investigation or adjudication of a claim involving that claimant or lawyer.

B. A Trustee with a past or present relationship, other than as provided in Paragraph A, with a claimant or the lawyer whose alleged conduct is the subject to the claim, or who has other potential conflicts of interest, shall disclose such relationship to the Board and, if the Board deems appropriate, that Trustee shall not participate in any proceeding relating to such claim.

Comment

[1] The Board must be sensitive to the perceptions of both the public and the legal profession in its determination of claims. Disqualification of members of the Board tainted by real or apparent conflicts of interest helps to ensure confidence in the impartiality in the proceeding. Potential conflicts of interest that should be disclosed include relations with other parties, such as with potential third-party sources of recovery.

Rule 9. Immunity

The Trustees, employees and agents of the Board shall be absolutely immune from civil liability for all acts in the course of their official duties. Absolute immunity shall also extend to claimants and lawyers who assist claimants for all communications to the Fund.

Comment

[1] Immunity from civil liability encourages lawyers and members of the public to serve on the Board and protects their independent judgment in the evaluation of claims. Immunity also protects the fiscal integrity of the Fund, and encourages claimants and lawyers to participate in seeking reimbursement for eligible losses.

[2] As a matter of public policy, immunity should attach to the Fund's activities and proceedings in the same way that absolute immunity attaches in lawyer disciplinary proceedings.

[3] In the absence of court rule or statute, immunity may not be available in proceedings involving voluntary funds. Insurance may therefore be required to protect Trustees, staffs, claimants, and the volunteer lawyers who assist claimants in processing their claims.

Rule 10. Eligible Claims

A. An eligible loss must be caused by the dishonest conduct of the lawyer in the practice of law and shall have arisen out of and by reason of a client-lawyer relationship or a fiduciary relationship between the lawyer and the claimant.

B. The claim shall have been filed no later than five years after the loss occurred or five years after the claimant knew or should have reasonable discovered the dishonest conduct of the lawyer.

C. As used in these Rules, "dishonest conduct" means wrongful acts committed by a lawyer in the nature of theft or embezzlement of money or the wrongful taking or conversion of money, property or other things of value, including but not limited to:

(1) failure to refund unearned fees received in advance as required by [Rule 1.16(d) of the ABA *Model Rules for Professional Conduct*]; and

(2) the borrowing of money from a client without intention to repay it, or with disregard of the lawyer's inability or reasonably anticipated inability to repay it.

D. Except as provided by Paragraph E of this Rule, the following losses shall not be reimbursable:

(1) losses incurred by spouses, children, parents, grandparents, siblings, partners, associates and employees of lawyer(s) causing the losses;

(2) losses covered by a bond, surety agreement, or insurance contract to the extent covered thereby, including any loss to which any bonding agent, surety or insurer is subrogated, to the extent of that subrogated interest;

(3) losses incurred by any financial institution that are recoverable under a "banker's blanket bond" or similar commonly available insurance or surety contract;

(4) losses incurred by any business entity controlled by the lawyer(s), any person or entity described in Subparagraph D (1), (2) or (3) of this Rule;

(5) losses incurred by any governmental entity or agency;

(6) losses arising from business or personal investments not arising from the practice of law or in the course of the client-lawyer relationship; and

(7) consequential or incidental damages, such as lost interest, or lawyer's fees or other costs incurred in seeking recovery of a loss.

E. In determining whether it would be more appropriate for this Fund or another Fund to pay a claim, the Board should consider the following factors:

(1) the Fund(s) into which the lawyer is required to pay an annual assessment or into which an appropriation is made on behalf of the lawyer by the bar association;

(2) the domicile of the lawyer;

(3) the domicile of the client;

(4) the residence(s) of the lawyer;

(5) the number of years the lawyer has been licensed or authorized to practice in each jurisdiction;

(6) the location of the lawyer's principal office and other offices;

(7) the location where the client lawyer relationship arose;

(8) the primary location where the legal services were rendered;

(9) whether at the time the legal services were rendered, the lawyer was engaged in the unauthorized practice of law as defined by the jurisdiction in which the legal services were rendered; and

(10) any other significant contacts.

F. The Board may enter into an agreement with the Fund of another jurisdiction to reimburse a portion of the loss suffered by a claimant whose claim may be eligible for payment under both Funds. The Board may take into consideration the other Fund's rules on payment of claims for reimbursement prior to entering into such an agreement.

G. In cases of extreme hardship or special and unusual circumstances, the Board may, in its discretion and consistent with the purpose of the Fund, recognize a claim that would otherwise be excluded under these Rules.

H. In cases where it appears that there will be unjust enrichment, or the claimant unreasonably or knowingly contributed to the loss, the Board may, in its discretion, deny the claim.

Comment

[1] Set forth in Paragraph A is the basic criteria for compensability of losses. An eligible claim must include: (1) a demonstrable loss; (2) caused by the dishonest conduct of a lawyer in the practice of law; and (3) within or arising out of a client-lawyer or fiduciary relationship.

[2] Fiduciary relationships are included because lawyers traditionally serve in that capacity as executors, conservators and guardians *ad litem*. Rejection of claims based upon technical distinctions between this sort of service and a client-lawyer relationship would not serve the purpose or mission of the Fund.

[3] Paragraph C adds to the Rules a definition of "dishonest conduct." The basic concept is one of conversion or embezzlement. Subparagraphs (1) and (2) make clear that if the essential nature of the transaction was conversion, dishonest conduct will be found even where the lawyer took money in the guise of a fee, a loan or an investment. Indeed, employing such a ruse is part of the dishonesty. Subparagraph (1) sets forth a standard for the handling of difficult unearned fee claims in accordance

with Rule 1.16(d) of the ABA *Model Rules of Professional Conduct*. It is not intended to encompass bona fide fee disputes. Where money received by a lawyer was clearly neither earned nor returned, however, the client feels violated, hardship can result, and the Board may find dishonest conduct. Subparagraph (2) anticipates overreaching by a lawyer, in the context of a loan to the lawyer by the client, to such an egregious extent as to be tantamount to theft. Similarly, use by the lawyer of a purported "investment" to induce a client to turn over money should not preclude a finding of dishonest conduct where the "investment" is worthless, non-existent and so forth.

[4] Paragraph C must be read in light of Paragraph A. In focusing on dishonest conduct, it must be kept in mind that such conduct must occur within or as a result of a client-lawyer or fiduciary relationship in order to be compensable.

[5] A five-year limitation on the filing of claims from the date the claimant knew or should have reasonably discovered the dishonest conduct is contained in Paragraph B. Under Paragraph E, the Board should provide liberal leeway for extension, however, especially in light of the extent to which the Fund publicizes itself. It is not knowledge of the dishonest conduct but the lack of knowledge of the existence or purpose of the Fund that is the problem for many prospective claimants.

[6] Paragraph D describes claims that are not reimbursable. Subparagraphs (1), (4), and (5) declare certain classes of potential claimants to be ineligible for policy reasons. Subparagraphs (2) and (3) imply that recourse should be sought from certain third parties such as title insurance companies and banks cashing checks over forged endorsements prior to seeking it from the Fund. Such third parties lack the client-lawyer relationship necessary to prosecute a claim in their own right. Should such third parties fail or refuse to pay, the Fund should promptly pay the claim, take an assignment from the claimant, and pursue the third parties in its own right.

[7] Subparagraph D (6) addresses the most difficult of Fund claims. Claims in which lawyers steal from their clients in the guise of "investments" should be paid, but transactions having nothing to do with the lawyer's license to practice are not compensable. Claims with facts somewhere between the two extremes often arise, and the issue is whether there is "enough of" a client-lawyer relationship. The application of a "but for" test is helpful: "But for the lawyer enjoying a client-lawyer

relationship with the claimant, such loss could not have occurred." Factors considered in applying this test include (1) disparity in sophistication and bargaining power between lawyer and claimant; (2) extent to which client-lawyer relationship overcame the normal prudence of claimant; (3) extent to which lawyer became privy to claimant's financial information as claimant's lawyer; (4) whether the transaction originated with lawyer; (5) reputation of lawyer as to law practice or business involvements; (6) amount charged by lawyer for legal services as opposed to finder's fees; and (7) number, nature, and timing of prior transactions between claimant and lawyer.

[8] Paragraph E sets forth factors to be considered by the Board when deciding whether this Fund, another jurisdiction's Fund, or both Funds should pay a claim where more than one Fund has jurisdiction over a lawyer. This situation might arise where a lawyer is licensed in two or more jurisdictions; a lawyer is licensed in only one jurisdiction and has engaged in the authorized multijurisdictional practice of law in another jurisdiction; or a lawyer is licensed in only one jurisdiction and has engaged in the unlicensed practice of law in another jurisdiction. The factors are not listed in order of priority and each matter should be considered separately based on a totality of the circumstances and the factors present.

[9] Paragraph F recognizes that there may be situations where it is appropriate for the Board to enter into an agreement with the Fund of another jurisdiction to reimburse a portion of the loss suffered by a claimant whose claim may be eligible for payment under both Funds. However, since Funds have different maximum dollar amounts of reimbursement for individual losses, the Fund with a higher maximum amount should not be required in every case to contribute more than the other Fund, or to contribute the maximum amount. Such a requirement could result in an undue burden on the Fund. The Board may take into consideration the other Fund's rules and its own rules on payment of claims for reimbursement, as well as the factors in Paragraph (E), prior to entering into such an agreement.

[10] Paragraphs G and H reiterate the critical importance of vesting in the Board the discretion to do justice in each claim considered, without needlessly following technical rules. These paragraphs recognize that it is impossible to predict every factual circumstance that will be presented to the Board.

Rule 11. Procedures and Responsibilities for Claimants

A. The Board shall prepare and approve a form for claiming reimbursement.

B. The form shall include at least the following information provided by the claimant under penalty of perjury:

(1) the name and address of claimant, home and business telephone, occupation and employer, social security number;

(2) the name, address and telephone number of the lawyer alleged to have dishonestly taken the claimant's money or property, and any family or business relationship of the claimant to the lawyer;

(3) the legal or other fiduciary services the lawyer was to perform for the claimant;

(4) the amount paid to the lawyer;

(5) a copy of any written agreement pertaining to the claim;

(6) copies of any checks, money orders, receipts, or other proofs of payment;

(7) the form of the claimant's alleged loss (e.g. money, securities or other property);

(8) the amount of the alleged loss and the date when the loss occurred;

(9) the date when the claimant discovered the alleged loss, and how the claimant discovered the alleged loss;

(10) the lawyer's dishonest conduct and the names and addresses of any persons who have knowledge of the alleged loss;

(11) the name of the person, if any, to whom the loss has been reported (e.g. district attorney, police, disciplinary agency, or other person or entity) and a copy of any complaint and description of any action that was taken;

(12) any source, from which the alleged loss can be reimbursed including any insurance, fidelity or surety agreement;

(13) the description of any steps taken to recover the alleged loss directly from the lawyer, or any other source;

(14) the circumstances under which the claimant has been, or will be, reimbursed for any part of the claim (including the

amount received, or to be received, and the source); along with a statement that the claimant agrees to notify the Board of any reimbursements the claimant receives during the pendency of the claim;

(15) the existence of facts believed to be important to the Fund's consideration of the claim;

(16) the manner in which the claimant learned about the Fund;

(17) the name, address and telephone number of the claimant's present lawyer;

(18) the claimant's agreement to cooperate with the Board in reference to the claim or as required by Rule 16, in reference to civil actions which may be brought in the name of the Board pursuant to a subrogation and assignment clause which shall also be contained within the claim;

(19) the claimant's agreement to repay the Fund if the claimant is subsequently reimbursed from another source;

(20) the name and address of any other state Fund to which the claimant has applied or intends to apply for reimbursement, together with a copy of the application; and

(21) a statement that the claimant agrees to the publication of appropriate information about the nature of the claim and the amount of reimbursement if reimbursement is made.

C. The claimant shall have the responsibility to complete the claim form and provide satisfactory evidence of a reimbursable loss.

D. The claim shall be filed with the Board in the manner and place designated in the Board's rules.

Comment

[1] The Board is required to develop a claim form for claimants to establish their eligibility for reimbursement. The form should be comprehensive enough to minimize the investigative burden of the Board, yet not so detailed as to discourage eligible claimants from applying for reimbursement.

[2] The enumeration in Paragraph B has been developed from claim forms in current use in several jurisdictions. Local need may require the enumeration to be supplemented by the Board. See also, Paragraph A of Rule 18, which addresses confidentiality.

[3] Paragraph C assigns the ultimate burden of establishing eligibility for reimbursement upon the claimant. No formal or technical quantum of proof is imposed on the claimant or the Board, but a preponderance of evidence is recommended. In many cases, of course, the lawyers' dishonest conduct will already have been established in a lawyer discipline action upon the "clear and convincing evidence" standard or, "beyond a reasonable doubt" in a criminal proceeding involving the same facts which constitute the claim for reimbursement. (See, Rule 18C of the ABA *Model Rules for Lawyer Disciplinary Enforcement.*)

Rule 12. Processing Claims

A. When it appears that a claim is not eligible for reimbursement pursuant to Rule 10, the claimant shall be advised of the reasons why the claim may not be eligible for reimbursement, and that unless additional facts to support eligibility are submitted to the Fund, the claim file shall be closed.

B. An order disciplining a lawyer for the same dishonest act or conduct alleged in a claim, or a final judgment imposing civil or criminal liability therefor, shall be evidence that the lawyer committed such dishonest act or conduct.

C. The lawyer disciplinary authority shall be promptly notified of the claim and required to furnish a report of its investigation of the matter to the Board. The lawyer disciplinary agency shall allow the Fund's representative access to its records during an investigation of a claim. The Board shall evaluate whether the investigation is complete and determine whether the Board should conduct additional investigation or await the pendency of any disciplinary investigation or proceeding involving the same act or conduct that is alleged in the claim.

D. The Board may conduct its own investigation when it deems it appropriate.

E. A lawyer who is the subject of a claim for reimbursement shall be notified of the claim and given an opportunity to respond to the claim. A copy of the claim shall be provided to the lawyer, or the lawyer's representative. The lawyer or representative shall have 20 days in which to respond.

F. The Board may request that testimony be presented to complete the record. Upon request, the claimant or lawyer, or their representatives, will be given an opportunity to be heard.

G. The Board may make a finding of dishonest conduct for purposes of adjudicating a claim. Such a determination is not a finding of dishonest conduct for purposes of professional discipline.

H. When the record is complete, the claim shall be determined on the basis of all available evidence, and notice shall be given to the claimant and the lawyer of the Board's determination and the reasons therefor. The approval or denial of a claim shall require the affirmative votes of at least four trustees.

I. Any proceeding upon a claim need not be conducted according to technical rules relating to evidence, procedure and witnesses. Any relevant evidence shall be admitted if it is the type of evidence upon which responsible persons are accustomed to rely in the conduct of serious affairs, regardless of the existence of any common law or statutory rule which might make improper the admission of such evidence over objection in court proceedings. The claimant shall have the duty to supply relevant evidence to support the claim.

J. The Board shall determine the order and manner of payment and pay all approved claims, but unless the Board directs otherwise, no claim should be approved during the pendency of a disciplinary proceeding involving the same act or conduct that is alleged in the claim.

Comment

[1] Rule 12 addresses the procedure for consideration of a claim in concert with the disciplinary process. The overall scheme presented is one of cooperation between the Fund and disciplinary authorities pursuant to Paragraph C, while avoiding duplication of effort in Paragraph B but respecting the different needs and autonomous functioning of the respective bodies identified in Paragraphs D and G.

[2] The Rule also seeks to set forth a framework which balances the Fund's duty to address the claimant's allegations efficiently with the need to present the respondent lawyer with an opportunity to defend pursuant to Paragraphs E, F and H.

[3] The overriding policy implicit in Rule 12 is that the Board exercises its discretion so as to make the best possible decision as expeditiously as possible in each claim presented. The Board may conduct any investigation it deems appropriate under Paragraph D, including the taking of testimony pursuant to Paragraph F. Paragraph J provides that the order and manner of payment of claims is likewise within the Board's discretion. Paragraph H requires the Board to articulate to each side the rationale for its determination on a given claim. Under Paragraph I, technical rules of evidence shall not be employed to hinder the Board from accomplishing its mission.

[4] Note that under Paragraph H the affirmative vote of at least four Trustees is required in order to dispose of a claim, just as it is for any matter before the Board under Rule 6C. Thus, for example, if the minimum necessary for a quorum is present, any motion that cannot garner unanimous support will fail. A "majority of the quorum present" will not suffice. This Paragraph does not prevent determinations of claims by mail ballot.

[5] Ideally the initial investigation should be done by the lawyer disciplinary agency personnel to avoid duplication of effort and inconsistent findings of both entities. The financial integrity of the Fund is preserved by using existing resources. Investigation by the Board should be utilized to gather additional evidence or to provide evidence in those jurisdictions where the discipline agency is unable to timely reveal the results of the investigation.

[6] As noted in the Comment to Rule 11, in many matters, a criminal conviction or a finding during disciplinary proceedings will establish "dishonest conduct" for purposes of the Board's determination of the claim. A discipline or other agency may, however, lack jurisdiction or have little incentive to act where the lawyer is unlikely to engage in further misconduct. This dilemma is illustrated by lawyers who have died, become mentally or physically incapacitated, fled the jurisdiction, or been disciplined for other reasons. The Board may then be required under Paragraph G to make a finding of dishonest conduct based on a preponderance of the evidence solely for the purpose of the Fund's proceeding.

[7] The Fund should have professional staff to assist the Board in investigating claims. Volunteers often cannot devote the same time and attention as staff members.

[8] The Fund's investigations should be augmented by subpoena power, consistent with the local rules of civil procedure. While a claimant

has the burden of providing satisfactory evidence of a reimbursable loss under Paragraph C of Rule 11, the Board should be given the opportunity to make the best possible decision on each matter before it.

Rule 13. Request for Reconsideration

The claimant or respondent may request reconsideration in writing within 30 days of the denial or determination of the amount of a claim. If the claimant or respondent fails to make a request or the request is denied, the decision of the Board is final and there is no further right or appeal.

Comment

[1] This Rule establishes a procedure to provide an opportunity for reconsideration of a claim. It permits claimants or respondents further consideration without creating a right of appeal or judicial review. The opportunity for reconsideration also provides a safeguard against dismissal of a claim not fully presented earlier.

Rule 14. Payment of Claims for Reimbursement

A. **The Board may from time to time fix a maximum amount on reimbursement that is payable by the Fund.**

B. **Payment of reimbursement shall be made in such amounts and at such times as the Board deems appropriate and may be paid in lump sum or installment amounts.**

C. **If a claimant is a minor or has otherwise been found to lack the capacity to receive and manage funds on their own behalf, the reimbursement may be paid to any person or entity authorized to receive the reimbursement for the benefit of the claimant.**

Comment

[1] Full reimbursement is the goal of a Fund, and adequate financing is essential to its achievement. Realistically, however, this ideal must be tempered with a Fund's need to provide all eligible claimants with meaningful, if not total, reimbursement for their losses.

[2] A maximum limitation on reimbursement permits the assets of a developing Fund to accumulate while an historical "claims presented"

record is established. It also serves to protect established Funds from catastrophic losses. Toward that end, Paragraph A authorizes the Board to fix a maximum limitation on reimbursement, whether for individual losses, or for the aggregate for all losses sustained by the clients of an individual lawyer.

[3] An aggregate limitation is permitted under Paragraph A, but it is not encouraged. An aggregate limitation has the potential of unfairness and is inconsistent with the goal of providing full reimbursement to all eligible claimants. Unless clearly required by a new and developing Fund, it should not be utilized. When utilized, the Board should aim for its elimination as soon as the Fund's fiscal conditions permit.

[4] Maximum limitations, whether individual or aggregate, should be reviewed periodically in light of the Fund's actual experience in providing reimbursement to eligible claimants for their documented losses.

[5] Paragraph B assigns responsibility for the determination of the actual amount of each reimbursement to the discretion of the Board.

[6] Paragraph B also grants the Board flexibility in paying reimbursement. Depending on a Fund's financial and administrative needs, periodic payment dates can be established, and reimbursement can be paid in lump sums or in installments.

[7] Similarly, where losses involve minors and individuals who have been placed under financial guardianship/conservatorship, Paragraph C permits the Board to pay the reimbursement directly to a parent or legal representative, for the benefit of the claimant.

Rule 15. Reimbursement from the Fund is Discretionary

No person shall have the legal right to reimbursement from the Fund. There shall be no appeal from the final decision of the Board.

Comment

[1] Although these Rules establish procedures for the processing of claims seeking reimbursement from the Fund, they are not intended to create either substantive rights to reimbursement, compensation, damages or restitution for a lawyer's dishonest conduct, or procedural rights subject to judicial review with respect to determination of claims.

[2] The Fund is not a guarantor of honesty and integrity in the practice of law. Dishonest conduct by a member of the bar imposes no separate legal obligation on the profession collectively, or on the Fund, to compensate for a lawyer's misconduct. The Fund is a lawyer-financed public service, and payments by the Board is discretionary.

Rule 16. Restitution and Subrogation

A. A lawyer whose dishonest conduct results in reimbursement to a claimant shall be liable to the Fund for restitution; and the Board may bring such action as it deems advisable to enforce such obligation.

B. A lawyer whose dishonest conduct has resulted in reimbursement to a claimant shall be obligated to make restitution to the Fund including interest and the expenses incurred by the Fund in processing the claim. A lawyer's failure to make full restitution or a satisfactory arrangement for restitution shall be cause for suspension, disbarment, or denial of an application for reinstatement.

C. As a condition of reimbursement, and to the extent of the reimbursement provided by the Fund, a claimant shall be required to provide the Fund with a transfer of the claimant's rights against the lawyer, the lawyer's legal representative, estate or assigns; and of the claimant's rights against any third party or entity who may be liable for the claimant's loss.

D. Upon commencement of an action by the Board as subrogee or assignee of a claim, it shall advise the claimant, who may then join in such action to recover the claimant's unreimbursed losses, if any.

E. In the event that the claimant commences an action to recover unreimbursed losses against the lawyer or another entity that may be liable for the claimant's loss, the claimant shall be required to notify the Board of such action.

F. The claimant shall be required to agree to cooperate in all efforts that the Board undertakes to achieve restitution for the Fund, and to repay the Fund if claimant is subsequently reimbursed from another source an amount that exceeds the difference between the principal misappropriated and the Fund award. Such repayment shall not exceed the amount of the Fund award.

Comment

[1] As fiduciaries of the Fund, the Board has the obligation to seek restitution, in appropriate cases, for reimbursement paid to claimants. Successful restitution efforts can enlarge the Fund's financial capacity to provide reimbursement to eligible claimants, and also reduce the need to increase assessments on lawyers to finance the operations of the Fund.

[2] The Board may seek restitution by direct legal action against the lawyer, as well as by the enforcement of rights provided by subrogation and assignment against the lawyer, the lawyer's estate, or any other person or entity who may be liable for the claimant's loss.

[3] Paragraph A is a statement of the Fund's right to seek restitution from the lawyer whose dishonest conduct resulted in a payment of reimbursement. Paragraph A creates an obligation on the dishonest lawyer to reimburse the Fund for all payments made by the Fund to the lawyer's clients. Under Paragraph B, the making of restitution to the Fund by the dishonest lawyer is a condition precedent to the lawyer's continued practice of law.

[4] Paragraph C requires the Board to establish a subrogation policy that requires claimants who receive reimbursement from the Fund to contractually transfer to the Fund their rights against the lawyer and any other person or entity that may be liable for the loss which the Fund reimbursed. This ordinary transfer of rights by subrogation is to extent of the reimbursement provided by the Fund.

[5] Paragraphs D and E provide for appropriate notice and joinder of parties in subrogation actions by the Fund, or by a claimant, where the claimant has received less than full reimbursement from the Fund.

[6] Paragraph F requires a claimant agree to cooperate with the Fund in its efforts to secure restitution.

[7] The provisions of Paragraphs C, D, E, and F will ordinarily be incorporated in the Fund's subrogation agreement with the claimant.

[8] Subrogation agreements should be carefully drawn to maximize the Board's creditor rights. In appropriate cases, subrogation should be supplemented with a full or partial assignment of specific rights possessed by a claimant, such as a payee's rights as a party to a negotiable instrument, or as a judgment creditor.

[9] The Board should seek the enactment of local law, if necessary, to enhance the Fund's creditors rights. One example is a statutory grant of subrogation rights once the Fund reimburses a claimant's loss. A statutory

right of subrogation can effectively supplement contractual subrogation, and may eliminate the need for individual agreements.

[10] Another enhancement that local law might provide a Fund is an automatic lien upon payment of restitution. The lien can serve a two-fold purpose: enabling the Board to intercept restitution which the lawyer is obligated to pay a claimant and preventing claimants from receiving double payments for their losses.

[11] Although most collection efforts directly against the lawyer will not be immediately successful as a practical matter, it is important that the Fund acquire the claimant's rights when it pays reimbursement. A transfer of rights has the potential for a later recoupment of restitution, and to prevent a claimant's double recovery for the same loss.

[12] Lawyer disciplinary agencies, increasingly require lawyers to make restitution to Funds, or to clients, as a condition of discipline or for reinstatement to practice. *See,* ABA *Model Rules for Lawyer Disciplinary Enforcement.*

[13] The Board, through the exercise of subrogation and assignments rights, can also recover restitution from collateral sources, including law partners.

Rule 17. Judicial Relief

A. The Board may make application to the appropriate court for relief to protect the interests of claimants or the Fund where:

(1) the assets of clients appear to be in danger of misappropriation or loss;

(2) to secure the claimant's or Fund's rights to restitution or subrogation; or

(3) where the lawyer has not been disciplined

B. A court's jurisdiction in such proceedings shall include the authority to appoint and compensate custodial receivers to conserve the assets and practices of disciplined, missing, incapacitated and deceased lawyers.

Comment

[1] Paragraph A subsection c allows the Board to take action to protect the claimant's interest in matters where the disciplinary authority has not taken action against the lawyer. This often arises in claims from the

former clients of deceased lawyers or lawyers who have been permanently disbarred for similar conduct. Though further discipline is not possible in such matters, the claims arising from them may still be valid. It is important that the Board have the ability the protect the interests of claimants and the Fund in these types of claims.

[2] Occasionally a situation arises in which the protection of clients and the Fund requires the appointment of a custodial receiver to wind down the practice and to preserve assets. Rule 17 makes explicit the Board's authority to seek just such a remedy as is available under state law. It is anticipated that the Rule would be adapted to seeking equitable remedies in each jurisdiction.

RULE 18. CONFIDENTIALITY

A. Claims, proceedings and reports involving claims for reimbursement are confidential until the Board authorizes reimbursement to the claimant, except as provided below, unless provided otherwise by law. After payment of the reimbursement, the Board shall publicize the nature of the claim, the amount of reimbursement, and the name of the lawyer. The name and the address of the claimant shall not be publicized by the Board unless specific permission has been granted by the claimant.

B. This Rule shall not be construed to deny access to relevant information by lawyer disciplinary authorities or other law enforcement authorities as the Board shall authorize, or the release of statistical information that does not disclose the identity of the lawyer or the parties, or the use of such information as is necessary to pursue the Fund's subrogation rights under Rule 16.

Comment

[1] The need to protect wrongly accused lawyers and to preserve the independence of the Board's deliberations should be balanced with the strong public interest in protecting legal consumers and promoting public confidence in the administration of justice.

[2] Publication of awards by the Board demonstrates the legal profession's responsiveness to clients and its commitment to self-regulation.

Responsible public information programs are essential to achieving the purposes of the Fund. The public, bar, and judicial leaders, and the news media should be kept informed of the activities of the Board and the status of its reimbursement efforts.

[3] The Board must also be sensitive to the privacy concerns of claimants, and of the constitutional rights of lawyers who may be the subject of criminal proceedings. Deferring publicity may therefore be appropriate where there is a pending criminal prosecution against a lawyer. Securing a claimant's consent to the release of information concerning a claimant's loss and reimbursement may also be a desirable practice, particularly for a voluntary fund which may not be protected by the immunity that is afforded a court-established Fund under Rule 9.

[4] It is within the discretion of the Board to determine which public agencies should be provided access to claim files. Lawyer discipline, law enforcement, and agencies considering nominations to public offices may have a legitimate need for information contained in the Fund's records that would otherwise be confidential.

Rule 19. Compensation for Representing Claimants

No lawyer shall charge or accept any payment for assisting a claimant with prosecuting a claim, unless such payment has been approved by the Board.

Comment

[1] Proceedings to determine claims are not necessarily adversarial in nature, and Fund employees should be available to assist claimants in understanding and preparing claims forms. The Bar should be encouraged to assist claimants as a particularly appropriate form of *pro bono* service, and appreciation for such work ought to be expressed.

ABA MODEL RULES FOR TRUST ACCOUNT OVERDRAFT NOTIFICATION

Adopted by the American Bar Association House of Delegates on February 9, 1988.

American Bar Association
Standing Committee on Lawyers' Responsibility for Client Protection
1987–1988

Honorable William R. Robie, *Chair*
Falls Church, Virginia

Robert L. Burkett
Los Angeles, California

Isaac Hecht
Baltimore, Maryland

I.S. Leevy Johnson
Columbia, South Carolina

Paul M. Larson
Yakima, Washington

Gail A. Lione
Baltimore, Maryland

Frederick Miller
Albany, New York

Herbert M. Rosenthal
San Francisco, California

Harry Zukernick
Miami, Florida

Honorable William R. Goldberg, *Liaison*
ABA Board of Governors
Providence, Rhode Island

American Bar Association
Advisory Commission on Client Security Funds
1987–1988

Kenneth J. Bossong, *Chair*
Trenton, New Jersey

Bobby E. James
Raleigh, North Carolina

Jerome F. O'Rourke
Flint, Michigan

Richard Reimers
Scottsdale, Arizona

William D. Ricker, Jr.
Fort Lauderdale, Florida

Sarah Singer
Boston, Massachusetts

Kiyoko Tatsui
Los Angeles, California

Center for Professional Responsibility

Director
Jeanne P. Gray

Assistant Client Protection Counsel
Gilbert A. Webb

MODEL RULES FOR TRUST ACCOUNT OVERDRAFT NOTIFICATION

PREFACE

The rules of professional conduct mandate and the lawyer disciplinary systems enforce the standard of safekeeping of client property as a fundamental fiduciary obligation of lawyers. The dishonor of drafts for insufficient funds drawn from client trust accounts is an "early warning" that a lawyer is engaging in conduct likely to injure clients. An overdraft notification program has the potential to reduce significantly the level of lawyer defalcations across the country. By requiring financial institutions which maintain lawyer trust accounts to notify the highest court or lawyer disciplinary agency of overdrafts, the appropriate disciplinary authorities are able to intervene before major losses occur and significant number of clients are harmed. The rule also enables authorities to counsel errant lawyers to take corrective action before the lawyer's misconduct becomes so egregious as to mandate serious sanction. Participation by financial institutions is a prerequisite to their continued eligibility to hold lawyer trust accounts. The costs of providing notification can be assessed against the lawyer who caused the overdraft. An effective overdraft notification program should conserve substantial resources for both clients and lawyers' funds for client protection.

Rule 1. Clearly Identified Trust Accounts Required

Lawyers who practice law in this jurisdiction shall deposit all funds held in trust in this jurisdiction in accordance with [Rule 1.15(a) of the ABA *Model Rules of Professional Conduct*] in accounts clearly identified as "trust" or "escrow" accounts, referred to herein as "trust accounts," and shall take all steps necessary to inform the depository institution of the purpose and identity of such accounts. Funds held in trust include funds held in any fiduciary capacity in connection with a representation, whether as trustee, agent, guardian, executor or otherwise. Lawyer trust accounts shall be maintained only in financial institutions approved by the highest court of the jurisdiction or the state lawyer discipline agency.

Comment

[1] Under Rule 1.15(a) of the ABA *Model Rules of Professional Conduct* or its equivalent, a lawyer must maintain client funds in an account separate from the lawyer's own property. Trust funds for a lawyer's own spouse or minor child and a lawyer's own funds properly held in a nonfiduciary capacity, such as funds in a business or personal account, do not fall under this rule.

[2] It should be noted that although Rule of 1.15 generally requires that trust accounts be maintained in the state where the lawyer's office is situated, trust property may be held outside the lawyer's home jurisdiction upon consent of the client. The overdraft notification rule governs funds held within the adopting state. A lawyer's obligation to deposit trust funds in an approved institution will arise upon adoption of the overdraft notification rule in a state where the lawyer deposits trust funds, whether that state is the state wherein the lawyer's office is situated or some other state.

Rule 2. Overdraft Notification Agreement Required

A financial institution shall be approved as a depository for lawyer trust accounts if it shall file with the highest court of the jurisdiction or the state lawyer disciplinary agency an agreement, in a form provided by the court or disciplinary agency, to report to the

disciplinary agency in the event any properly payable instrument is presented against a lawyer trust account containing insufficient funds, irrespective of whether or not the instrument is honored. The court or disciplinary agency shall establish rules governing approval and termination of approved status for financial institutions, and shall annually publish a list of approved financial institutions.

No trust account shall be maintained in any financial institution which does not agree to make such reports. Any such agreement shall apply to all branches of the financial institution and shall not be canceled except upon [30] days notice in writing to the court or disciplinary agency.

Comment

[1] For purposes of this rule, each financial institution wishing to be approved as a depository of client trust funds must file an overdraft notification agreement with the highest court or the jurisdiction. In some jurisdictions, the court may wish to delegate to the state bar or some other agency the duty to enter into overdraft notification agreements with financial institutions and to publish a list of approved institutions.

[2] The overdraft notification agreement requires that all overdrafts be reported to the state lawyer disciplinary agency, irrespective of whether or not the instrument is honored. In light of the purposes of this rule, and the ethical proscriptions concerning the preservation of client funds and commingling of client and lawyer funds, it would be improper for a lawyer to accept "overdraft privileges" or any other arrangement for a personal loan on a lawyer trust account.

[3] Denial of discretion to financial institutions serves two important purposes. First, it makes notification by a financial institution an administratively simple matter. An institution which receives an instrument for payment against insufficient funds need not evaluate whether circumstances require that notification be given; it merely provides notice. It then becomes the responsibility of the lawyer disciplinary agency to determine whether further action is warranted.

[4] Second, mandatory notification shields the financial institution from potential tort claims by the lawyer's clients for failure to report overdrafts. Liability for negligence in reporting overdrafts could be alleged by a person, injured by such failure to report, who falls within the zone of foreseeability

and for whose benefit the duty to report was instituted. Arguably, a financial institution could owe a duty to the lawyer's clients who supplied the funds, and to the lawyers' fund for client protection if a pay-out is made in the event of theft of those funds. If an institution reports all overdrafts, its potential liability for negligent failure to report is minimized. In cases where a bounced check or overdrafts is a result of an accounting error (caused by either the lawyer or the financial institution), but notification has already been sent to the state agency, the institution should provide the lawyer with a written explanation (preferably, an affidavit from an officer of the institution) which the lawyer can then submit to the agency to verify the error. In the event of financial institution error no record need be kept by the agency.

[5] The rule calls for the highest court of the jurisdiction (or lawyer disciplinary agency, where the court has so delegated) to establish rules governing approval of financial institutions' holding of client trust funds, and termination of such approved status. These rules should specify under what circumstances approved status will be withdrawn. For instance, the court's rules might state that approved status may be revoked where the institution demonstrates "a pattern of neglect or a showing of bad faith" rather than an occasional or negligent failure to report an overdraft.

Rule 3. Overdraft Reports

The overdraft notification agreement shall provide that all reports made by the financial institution shall be in the following format:

(1) In the case of a dishonored instrument, the report shall be identical to the overdraft notice customarily forwarded to the depositor, and should include a copy of the dishonored instrument, if such a copy is normally provided to depositors; and

(2) In the case of instruments that are presented against insufficient funds but which instruments are honored, the report shall identify the financial institution, the lawyer or law firm, the account number, the date of presentation for payment and the date paid, as well as the amount of overdraft created thereby.

Such reports shall be made simultaneously with, and within the time provided by law for, notice of dishonor, if any. If an instrument presented against insufficient funds is honored, then the report shall be made within [5] banking days of the date of presentation for payment against insufficient funds.

Comment

[1] The rule provides the proper format for overdraft reports, distinguishing between dishonored instruments and instruments that are presented against insufficient funds but honored. Where instruments are dishonored, a copy of the notice of dishonor is sufficient. Where instruments are presented against insufficient funds but paid, the rule specifies the information that the institution should provide.

[2] Ordinarily, a financial institution gives notice of an overdraft to a depositor before midnight of the next banking day following receipt of the item or notice. *See* Uniform Commercial Code (U.L.A.) § 3-503(c) (Revised Article 3, 1990) or Uniform Commercial Code (U.L.A.) § 3-508(2) (Prior Article 3, pre-1990). This is the same time period in which overdraft notification is to be given to the state lawyer disciplinary agency. Where an instrument presented against insufficient funds is honored, the rule recommends that the financial institution send overdraft notification to the agency within [5] days of the date of presentation.

[3] The rule contemplates that the lawyer disciplinary agency, upon receipt of the overdraft notification, will contact the lawyer or law firm by telephone and request an explanation for the overdraft. A letter, requesting a documented explanation, may also be sent. If the overdraft is an accounting error, the lawyer or law firm will submit a written, documented explanation to substantiate the error.

[4] Where the lawyer or law firm cannot supply an adequate or complete explanation for the overdraft, other action may be taken, including an audit or a demand for production of the lawyer's books and records.

Rule 4. Consent by Lawyers

Every lawyer practicing or admitted to practice in this jurisdiction shall, as a condition thereof, be conclusively deemed to have consented to the reporting and production requirements mandated by this rule.

Comment

[1] The rule establishes that consent to the reporting and production requirements mandated by the rule is a condition of the privilege to practice law in the jurisdiction which has adopted the rule. As a consequence, financial institutions are protected from claims by lawyer-depositors based

on disclosures made in accordance with the rule, although the only parties to an overdraft notification agreement are the court and the financial institution.

Rule 5. Costs

Nothing herein shall preclude a financial institution from charging a particular lawyer or law firm for the reasonable cost of producing the reports and records required by this rule.

Comment

[1] In addition to normal monthly maintenance fees on each account, the lawyer or law firm can anticipate that financial institutions will charge additional fees for reporting overdrafts in accordance with this rule.

[2] Financial institutions, however, already flag overdrafts and returned checks, and, thus, it is only slightly more burdensome for the institution to forward a copy to the state lawyer disciplinary agency. The additional cost to the lawyer should be insignificant.

[3] Rule 5 should not be interpreted to allow a lawyer to permit trust account funds to be reduced through deductions made by a financial institution to cover costs of overdraft notification. Notification costs, if charged, should not be borne by clients.

Rule 6. Definitions

"Financial institution" includes banks, savings and loan associations, credit unions, savings banks and any other business or person which accepts for deposit funds held in trust by lawyers.

"Properly payable" refers to an instrument which, if presented in the normal course of business, is in a form requiring payment under the laws of this jurisdiction.

"Notice of dishonor" refers to the notice which a financial institution is required to give, under the laws of this jurisdiction, upon presentation of an instrument which the institution dishonors.

Comment

[1] Under the laws of most jurisdictions, the definition of "properly payable" will be contained in Uniform Commercial Code (U.L.A.)

§ 4401(a) (Amended Article 4, 1990) ("An item is properly payable if it is authorized by the customer and is in accordance with any agreement between the customer and bank.") or its predecessor, Uniform Commercial Code (U.L.A.) § 4-104(i) (Prior Article 4, pre-1990) ("'Properly payable' includes the availability of funds for payment at the time of decision to pay or dishonor").

[2] Under the laws of most jurisdictions, the definition of "notice of dishonor" will be determined by reference to Uniform Commercial Code (U.L.A.) § 3-503(c) (Revised Article 3, 1990), under which notice must be given by a collecting bank before midnight of the next banking day following the banking day on which the bank receives notice of dishonor or by any other person within 30 days following the day on which the person receives notice of dishonor, or its predecessor, Uniform Commercial Code (U.L.A) § 3-508(2) (Prior Article 3, pre-1990), which states any necessary notice must be given by a bank before its midnight deadline and by any other person before midnight of the third business day after dishonor or receipt of notice of dishonor.

ABA MODEL RULES ON CLIENT TRUST ACCOUNT RECORDS

Adopted by the American Bar Association as the Model Rule & Financial Recordkeeping on February 3, 1993, and amended, as the Model Rules for Client Trust Account Records on August 9, 2010.

American Bar Association
Standing Committee on Client Protection
2009–2010

Honorable Daniel J. Crothers, *Chair*
Bismarck, North Dakota

Nancy L. Cohen
Denver, Colorado

Leo W. Ottey
Baltimore, Maryland

Michael E. Harmon
Little Rock, Arkansas

Jill A. Sperber
San Francisco, California

Janet Green Marbley
Columbus, Ohio

Charles J. Vigil
Albuquerque, New Mexico

Harold D. Pope, III, *Liaison*
ABA Board of Governors
Southfield, Michigan

Center for Professional Responsibility

Director
Jeanne P. Gray

Client Protection Counsel
John A. Holtaway

Associate Client Protection Counsel
Selina S. Thomas

MODEL RULES FOR CLIENT TRUST ACCOUNT RECORDS

Preface

Rule 1.15 of the ABA *Model Rules of Professional Conduct*, or its equivalent, requires that lawyers who are entrusted with the property of law clients and third persons in the practice of law must hold that property with the care required of a professional fiduciary. The basis for Rule 1.15 is the lawyer's fiduciary obligation to safeguard trust property, to segregate it from the lawyer's own property, and to avoid the appearance of impropriety.

Rule 1.15 specifically requires a lawyer to preserve "complete records" with respect to a law firm's trust accounts. It also obligates a lawyer to "promptly render a full accounting" for the receipt and distribution of trust property. A violation of Rule 1.15 may subject a lawyer to professional discipline. Rule 1.15 does not, however, provide lawyers or law firms with practical guidance in complying with these fiduciary obligations or in establishing basic accounting control systems for their law practices.

The *Model Rules for Client Trust Account Records* are intended to give further definition to the requirements of Rule 1.15. Adapted from existing court rules and incorporating both changes in banking laws and advances in technology that affect both norms in banking practice and lawyer practice, it proposes uniform and minimal standards for the maintenance of records related to client funds held in trust. These standards should guide lawyers and law firms, particularly those new to the practice of law.

Rule 1. Recordkeeping Generally

A lawyer who practices in this jurisdiction shall maintain current financial records as provided in these Rules and required by [Rule 1.15 of the Model Rules of Professional Conduct], and shall retain the following records for a period of [five years] after termination of the representation:

A. receipt and disbursement journals containing a record of deposits to and withdrawals from client trust accounts, specifically identifying the date, source, and description of each item deposited, as well as the date, payee and purpose of each disbursement;

B. ledger records for all client trust accounts showing, for each separate trust client or beneficiary, the source of all funds deposited, the names of all persons for whom the funds are or were held, the amount of such funds, the descriptions and amounts of charges or withdrawals, and the names of all persons or entities to whom such funds were disbursed;

C. copies of retainer and compensation agreements with clients [as required by Rule 1.5 of the Model Rules of Professional Conduct];

D. copies of accountings to clients or third persons showing the disbursement of funds to them or on their behalf;

E. copies of bills for legal fees and expenses rendered to clients;

F. copies of records showing disbursements on behalf of clients;

G. the physical or electronic equivalents of all checkbook registers, bank statements, records of deposit, pre-numbered canceled checks, and substitute checks provided by a financial institution;

H. records of all electronic transfers from client trust accounts, including the name of the person authorizing transfer, the date of transfer, the name of the recipient and confirmation from the financial institution of the trust account number from which money was withdrawn and the date and the time the transfer was completed;

I. copies of [monthly] trial balances and [quarterly] reconciliations of the client trust accounts maintained by the lawyer; and

J. copies of those portions of client files that are reasonably related to client trust account transactions.

Comment

[1] Rule 1 enumerates the basic financial records that a lawyer must maintain with regard to all trust accounts of a law firm. These include the standard books of account, and the supporting records that are necessary to safeguard and account for the receipt and disbursement of client or third person funds as required by Rule 1.15 of the Model Rules of Professional Conduct or its equivalent. Consistent with Rule 1.15, this Rule proposes that lawyers maintain client trust account records for a period of five years after termination of each particular legal engagement or representation. Although these Model Rules address the accepted use of a client trust account by a lawyer when holding client or third person funds, some jurisdictions may permit a lawyer to deposit certain advance fees for legal services into the lawyer's business or operating account. In those situations, the lawyer should still be guided by the standards contained in these Model Rules.

[2] Rule 1(g) requires that the physical or electronic equivalents of all checkbook registers, bank statements, records of deposit, pre-numbered canceled checks, and substitute checks be maintained for a period of five years after termination of each legal engagement or representation. The "Check Clearing for the 21st Century Act" or "Check 21 Act," codified at 12 U.S.C. § 5001 *et. seq.*, recognizes "substitute checks" as the legal equivalent of an original check. A "substitute check" is defined at 12 U.S.C. § 5002(16) as "paper reproduction of the original check that contains an image of the front and back of the original check; bears a magnetic ink character recognition ("MICR") line containing all the information appearing on the MICR line of the original check; conforms with generally applicable industry standards for substitute checks; and is suitable for automated processing in the same manner as the original check. Banks, as defined in 12 U.S.C. § 5002(2), are not required to return to customers the original canceled checks. Most banks now provide electronic images of checks to customers who have access to their accounts on internet-based websites. It is the lawyer's responsibility to download electronic images. Electronic images shall be maintained for the requisite number of years and shall be readily available for printing upon request or shall be printed and maintained for the requisite number of years.

[3] The ACH (Automated Clearing House) Network is an electronic funds transfer or payment system that primarily provides for the interbank clearing of electronic payments between originating and receiving

participating financial institutions. ACH transactions are payment instructions to either debit or credit a deposit account. ACH payments are used in a variety of payment environments including bill payments, business-to-business payments, and government payments (e.g. tax refunds.) In addition to the primary use of ACH transactions, retailers and third parties use the ACH system for other types of transactions including electronic check conversion (ECC). ECC is the process of transmitting MICR information from the bottom of a check, converting check payments to ACH transactions depending upon the authorization given by the account holder at the point-of-purchase. In this type of transaction, the lawyer should be careful to comply with the requirements of Rule 1(h).

[4] There are five types of check conversions where a lawyer should be careful to comply with the requirements of Rule 1(h). First, in a "point-of-purchase conversion," a paper check is converted into a debit at the point of purchase and the paper check is returned to the issuer. Second, in a "back-office conversion," a paper check is presented at the point of purchase and is later converted into a debit and the paper check is destroyed. Third, in an "account-receivable conversion," a paper check is converted into a debit and the paper check is destroyed. Fourth, in a "telephone-initiated debit" or "check-by-phone" conversion, bank account information is provided via the telephone and the information is converted to a debit. Fifth, in a "web-initiated debit," an electronic payment is initiated through a secure web environment. Rule 1(h) applies to each of the type of electronic funds transfers described. All electronic funds transfers shall be recorded and a lawyer should not re-use a check number which has been previously used in an electronic transfer transaction.

[5] The potential of these records to serve as safeguards is realized only if the procedures set forth in Rule 1(i) are regularly performed. The trial balance is the sum of balances of each client's ledger card (or the electronic equivalent). Its value lies in comparing it on a monthly basis to a control balance. The control balance starts with the previous month's balance, then adds receipts from the Trust Receipts Journal and subtracts disbursements from the Trust Disbursements Journal. Once the total matches the trial balance, the reconciliation readily follows by adding amounts of any outstanding checks and subtracting any deposits not credited by the bank at month's end. This balance should agree with the bank statement. Quarterly reconciliation is recommended only as a minimum requirement; monthly reconciliation is the preferred practice given the difficulty

of identifying an error (whether by the lawyer or the bank) among three months' transactions.

[6] In some situations, documentation in addition to that listed in paragraphs (a) through (i) of Rule 1 is necessary for a complete understanding of a trust account transaction. The type of document that a lawyer must retain under paragraph (j) because it is "reasonably related" to a client trust transaction will vary depending on the nature of the transaction and the significance of the document in shedding light on the transaction. Examples of documents that typically must be retained under this paragraph include correspondence between the client and lawyer relating to a disagreement over fees or costs or the distribution of proceeds, settlement agreements contemplating payment of funds, settlement statements issued to the client, documentation relating to sharing litigation costs and attorney fees for subrogated claims, agreements for division of fees between lawyers, guarantees of payment to third parties out of proceeds recovered on behalf of a client, and copies of bills, receipts or correspondence related to any payments to third parties on behalf of a client (whether made from the client's funds or from the lawyer's funds advanced for the benefit of the client).

Rule 2. Client Trust Account Safeguards

With respect to client trust accounts required by [Rule 1.15 of the Model Rules of Professional Conduct]:

A. only a lawyer admitted to practice law in this jurisdiction or a person under the direct supervision of the lawyer shall be an authorized signatory or authorize transfers from a client trust account;

B. receipts shall be deposited intact and records of deposit should be sufficiently detailed to identify each item; and

C. withdrawals shall be made only by check payable to a named payee and not to cash, or by authorized electronic transfer.

Comment

[1] Rule 2 enumerates minimal accounting controls for client trust accounts. It also enunciates the requirement that only a lawyer admitted to the practice of law in the jurisdiction or a person who is under the direct

supervision of the lawyer shall be the authorized signatory or authorize electronic transfers from a client trust account. While it is permissible to grant limited nonlawyer access to a client trust account, such access should be limited and closely monitored by the lawyer. The lawyer has a non-delegable duty to protect and preserve the funds in a client trust account and can be disciplined for failure to supervise subordinates who misappropriate client funds. See, Rules 5.1 and 5.3 of the Model Rules of Professional Conduct.

[2] Authorized electronic transfers shall be limited to (1) money required for payment to a client or third person on behalf of a client; (2) expenses properly incurred on behalf of a client, such as filing fees or payment to third persons for services rendered in connection with the representation; or (3) money transferred to the lawyer for fees that are earned in connection with the representation and are not in dispute; or (4) money transferred from one client trust account to another client trust account.

[3] The requirements in paragraph (b) that receipts shall be deposited intact mean that a lawyer cannot deposit one check or negotiable instrument into two or more accounts at the same time, a practice commonly known as a split deposit.

Rule 3. Availability of Records

Records required by Rule 1 may be maintained by electronic, photographic, or other media provided that they otherwise comply with these Rules and that printed copies can be produced. These records shall be readily accessible to the lawyer.

Comment

[1] Rule 3 allows the use of alternative media for the maintenance of client trust account records if printed copies of necessary reports can be produced. If trust records are computerized, a system of regular and frequent (preferably daily) back-up procedures is essential. If a lawyer uses third-party electronic or internet based file storage, the lawyer must make reasonable efforts to ensure that the company has in place, or will establish reasonable procedures to protect the confidentiality of client information. See, ABA Formal Ethics Opinion 398 (1995). Records required by Rule 1 shall be readily accessible and shall be readily available to be produced upon request by the client or third person who has an interest as provided

in Model Rule 1.15, or by the official request of a disciplinary authority, including but not limited to, a subpoena duces tecum. Personally identifying information in records produced upon request by the client or third person or by disciplinary authority shall remain confidential and shall be disclosed only in a manner to ensure client confidentiality as otherwise required by law or court rule.

[2] Rule 28 of the Model Rules for Lawyer Disciplinary Enforcement provides for the preservation of a lawyer's client trust account records in the event that the lawyer is transferred to disability inactive status, suspended, disbarred, disappears, or dies.

Rule 4. Dissolution of Law Firm

Upon dissolution of a law firm or of any legal professional corporation, the partners shall make reasonable arrangements for the maintenance of client trust account records specified in Rule 1.

Comment

[1] Rules 4 and 5 provide for the preservation of a lawyer's client trust account records in the event of dissolution or sale of a law practice. Regardless of the arrangements the partners or shareholders make among themselves for maintenance of the client trust records, each partner may be held responsible for ensuring the availability of these records. For the purposes of these Rules, the terms "law firm," "partner," and "reasonable" are defined in accordance with Rules 1.0(c),(g), and (h) of the Model Rules of Professional Conduct.

Rule 5. Sale of a Law Practice

Upon the sale of a law practice, the seller shall make reasonable arrangements for the maintenance of records specified in Rule 1.

ABA MODEL RULE FOR RANDOM AUDIT OF LAWYER TRUST ACCOUNTS

Adopted by the American Bar Association House of Delegates on August 11, 1993.

American Bar Association
Standing Committee on Lawyers' Responsibility for Client Protection
1992–1993

Ernest Y. Sevier, *Chair*
San Francisco, California

Pamela A. Bresnahan
Washington, D.C.

Kenneth J. Bossong
Trenton, New Jersey

James E. Green
Columbus, Ohio

Geoffrey C. Hazard, Jr.
New Haven, Connecticut

Isaac Hecht
Baltimore, Maryland

James F. Miller
Hollywood, Florida

Kiyoko Tatsui
Los Angeles, California

Harriet L. Turney
Phoenix, Arizona

Alex S. Keller, *Liaison*
ABA Board of Governors
Denver, Colorado

American Bar Association
Advisory Commission on Client Security Funds
1992–1993

Frederick Miller, *Chair*
Albany, New York

Brenda P. Catlett
Lake Oswego, Oregon

Mary Ann Cummings
Vancouver, British Columbia

Tricia W. Nagel
Philadelphia, Pennsylvania

Karen O'Toole
Boston, Massachusetts

David N. Shearon
Nashville, Tennessee

John C. Tillotson
Leavenworth, Kansas

Center for Professional Responsibility

Director
Jeanne P. Gray

Client Protection Counsel
David J. Brent

Assistant Client Protection Counsel
Gilbert A. Webb

MODEL RULE FOR RANDOM AUDIT OF LAWYER TRUST ACCOUNTS

PREFACE

This rule is predicated upon the adoption by the American Bar Association of Recommendation 16 of the Report of the Commission on Evaluation of Disciplinary Enforcement (the "McKay Commission"), which provided that random audits of lawyer trust accounts be authorized by court rule. The McKay Commission determined that random audits were a proven deterrent to the misuse of money and property in the practice of law and that examination of trust accounts by court-designated auditors provided practitioners with expert and practical assistance in maintaining necessary records and supporting books of account.

A. The [highest court of the jurisdiction] shall approve procedures to randomly select lawyer or law firm trust accounts for audit.

B. An audit of a lawyer or law firm trust account conducted pursuant to this rule shall be commenced by the issuance of an investigative subpoena to compel the production of records relating to a lawyer's or law firm's trust accounts. The subpoena shall contain a certification that it was issued in compliance with this rule, that the lawyer or law firm was selected at random, and that there exist no grounds to believe that professional misconduct has occurred with respect to the accounts being audited. The subpoena shall be served at least [10] business days before commencement of the audit.

C. With respect to each audit conducted pursuant to this rule, the examiner shall:

(1) determine whether the lawyer's or law firm's records and accounts are being maintained in accordance with applicable rules of court; and

(2) employ sampling techniques to examine "selected accounts," unless discrepancies are found which indicate a need for a more detailed audit. Selected accounts' may include money, securities and other trust assets held by the lawyer or law firm; safe deposit boxes and similar devices; deposit records; canceled checks or their equivalent; and any other

records which pertain to trust transactions affecting the lawyer's or law firm's practice of law.

D. The examiner shall prepare a written report containing the examiner's findings, a copy of which shall be provided to the audited lawyer or law firm.

E. In the event that the audit report asserts deficiencies in the audited lawyer's or law firm's records or procedures, the lawyer or law firm shall, within [10] business days after receipt of the report, provide evidence that the alleged deficiencies are incorrect, or that they have been corrected. If corrective action requires additional time, the lawyer or law firm shall apply for an extension of time to a date certain in which to correct the deficiencies cited in the audit report.

F. All records produced for an audit conducted pursuant to this rule shall remain confidential, and their contents shall not be disclosed in violation of the client-lawyer privilege.

G. Records produced for an audit conducted pursuant to this rule may be disclosed to:

(1) the lawyer disciplinary agency or to a court to the extent disclosure is necessary for the purposes of the particular audit;

(2) the lawyer disciplinary agency for the purposes of a disciplinary proceeding; and

(3) any other person, including a law enforcement agency, with the permission of the [highest court of the jurisdiction].

H. A lawyer or law firm shall cooperate in an audit conducted pursuant to this rule, and shall answer all questions pertaining thereto, unless the lawyer or law firm claims a privilege or right which is available to the lawyer or law firm under applicable state or federal law. A lawyer's or law firm's failure to cooperate in an audit conducted pursuant to this rule shall constitute professional misconduct.

I. No lawyer or law firm shall be subject to an audit conducted pursuant to this rule more frequently than once every [three] years.

Comment

[1] The rule proposes a basic structure and system for a random audit program, including such procedural safeguards as adequate prior notice before the commencement of an audit; written audit reports; the opportunity for an audited lawyer or law firm to respond to an examiner's report; the preservation of confidentiality of client records; and the frequency of audits conducted by random selection.

[2] The rule contemplates that assigned agencies will tailor or augment these basic procedures to address specific conditions, needs, and concerns which exist in their jurisdictions. Certain jurisdiction, for instance, issue an informal notice of audit rather than a subpoena. Such local rules require the assignment of administrative responsibility for the jurisdiction's random audit program to the lawyer disciplinary agency, the lawyers' fund for client protection, or other appropriate court-designated entity.

ABA MODEL RULE FOR PAYEE NOTIFICATION

Model Rule for Payee Notification

Adopted by the American Bar Association House of Delegates on August 13, 1991.

American Bar Association Standing Committee on Lawyers Responsibility for Client Protection 1990–1991

Herbert M. Rosenthal, *Chair*
San Francisco, California

Robert L. Burkett
Los Angeles, California

Kenneth J. Bossong
Trenton, New Jersey

Isaac Hecht
Baltimore, Maryland

John H. Neiman
Des Moines, Iowa

Richard H. Sinkfield
Atlanta, Georgia

Kiyoko Tatsui
Los Angeles, California

Elizabeth Michelman
Brookline, Massachusetts
Sherwin P. Simmons, *Liaison*
ABA Board of Governors
Tampa, Florida

American Bar Association Advisory Commission on Client Security Funds 1990–1991

Frederick Miller, *Chair*
Albany, New York

Marilyn Lindgren Cohen
Lake Oswego, Oregon

James E. Green
Columbus, Ohio

Bobby E. James
Raleigh, North Carolina

Tricia W. Nagel
Philadelphia, Pennsylvania

Jerome F. O'Rourke
Flint, Michigan

Karen O'Toole
Boston, Massachusetts

Mary Burns Tomlinson
Portland, Oregon

Center for Professional Responsibility

Director
Jeanne P. Gray

Client Protection Counsel
David J. Brent

Assistant Client Protection Counsel
Gilbert A. Webb

MODEL RULE FOR PAYEE NOTIFICATION

PREFACE

The *Model Rule for Payee Notification* is based upon Regulation 64 of the Department of Insurance of the State of New York, promulgated in 1988 (11 NYCRR 216.9 (A) & (B)), which requires notice to the payee in all insurance settlements in excess of $5,000. The regulation does not apply to no-fault payments from a claimant's own insurer. As implemented in various jurisdictions the provision for payee notification has been triggered by a dollar amount which ranges from $1,000 to $5,000.

In payment of liability claims, it is the customary practice of insurance carriers to deliver the settlement proceeds to the lawyer of record for the claimant, usually by check made payable jointly to the claimant and the claimant's lawyer. The underlying purpose for the practice is to protect and preserve the interests of all three parties to the transaction: the insured, the successful claimant and the claimant's lawyer. In the payment process, the insurance carrier does not typically notify the claimant when it makes payment to the claimant's lawyer or other representative. This gap in the process permits dishonest practices to interfere with the settlement and payment of insurance claims.

If the dishonest conduct involves the claimant's lawyer instances of lawyer misconduct can include the unauthorized settlement of the client's claim with the defendant's insurer, forgery of the claimant's signature on a stipulation of settlement or other legal document that may be required to complete the settlement, forgery of the claimant's endorsement on the settlement draft itself, or misappropriation of the claimant's share of the proceeds.

It is not uncommon for a dishonest lawyer to successfully conceal the unauthorized settlement and misappropriation for several years and to be unable to restore the claimant's funds when the loss is finally discovered. As few client protection funds are able to provide full reimbursement for all eligible losses, it is important that the legal profession devise and support methods of reducing losses resulting from dishonest conduct in the practice of law, including the misappropriation of personal injury settlements.

Experience in New York and other states demonstrates that the payee notification rule has had a salutary effect on lawyer misconduct, has demonstrated an effective protection device for clients and has benefitted the state lawyers' fund for client protection. A similar statute or regulation should have the same beneficial effect in other jurisdictions.

Written Notice to Claimants of Payment of Claims in Third Party Settlements.

A. **Upon the payment of [insert desired dollar amount] or more in settlement of any third-party liability claim, the insurer shall provide written notice to the claimant where: (1) the claimant is a natural person, and (2) the payment is delivered to the claimant's lawyer or other representative by draft, check or otherwise. Such notice shall be required when payment is made to a claimant by the insurer or its representative, including the insurer's lawyer.**

B. **This Rule shall not create any cause of action for any person against the insurer, other than a government agency, based upon the insurer's failure to provide notice to a claimant as required by this Rule; nor shall this Rule create a defense for any party to any cause of action based upon the insurer's failure to provide such notice.**

Comment

[1] This Rule is intended to serve as a deterrent to the dishonest conduct of a claimant's lawyer with respect to the receipt of third-party liability claims. The intended salutary effects of including the payee in the claim payment process should obtain whether the Rule is enacted as a statute or a regulation.

[2] The written notice requirement of Paragraph A of this Rule is reasonable and appropriate to advise the claimant of settlement of its liability claim by payment to its lawyer or other representative. Written notice provides the claimant with an independent and verifiable source of information concerning the facts of the settlement. It also provides the adverse party and insurer with certainty that the settlement has been concluded in a lawful manner.

[3] The provisions of Paragraph B are intended to make clear that an insurance carrier's failure to comply with this rule does not create a new cause of action or defense for a party. The insurer, however, may be subject to appropriate action by a state regulatory or licensing agency.

ABA MODEL RULES FOR FEE ARBITRATION

Adopted by the American Bar Association House of Delegates on February 6, 2012.

American Bar Association Standing Committee on Client Protection 2011–2012

Janet Green Marbley, *Chair*
Columbus, Ohio

Nancy Cohen
Denver, Colorado

Lindsey Draper
Madison, Wisconsin

Daniel Hendi
Trenton, New Jersey

Denzil McKenzie
Boston, Massachusetts

Leo Wesley Ottey Jr.
Baltimore, Maryland

Julia Smeds Roth
Decatur, Alabama

Justice Daniel J. Crothers, *Special Liasion*
Bismarck, South Dakota

Joseph Roszkowski, *Liaison*
ABA Board of Governors
Woonsocket, Rhode Island

Center for Professional Responsibility

Director
Jeanne P. Gray

Client Protection Counsel
Selina S. Thomas

MODEL RULES FOR FEE ARBITRATION

PREFACE

The Model Rules for Fee Arbitration implement Recommendation 3 of the Report of the Commission on Evaluation of Disciplinary Enforcement (the "McKay Commission," February 1992) in which the American Bar Association called for states to expand their systems of lawyer regulation by establishing mechanisms to resolve disputes between lawyers and clients and to handle non-disciplinary complaints about lawyers. The McKay Commission included a mandatory fee arbitration program its court-established dispute resolution mechanisms The rules were amended in February 2012 to reflect the evolution of Fee Arbitration programs to refine current practices in order to increase productivity, efficiency, and fairness.

Rule 1. General Principles and Jurisdiction

A. Definitions. The following definitions shall apply in all fee arbitration proceedings:

(1) "Client" means a person or entity who directly or through an authorized representative consults, retains or secures legal service or advice from a lawyer in the lawyer's professional capacity.

(2) "Commission" means the Fee Arbitration Commission.

(3) "Decision" means the determination made by the panel in a fee arbitration proceeding.

(4) "Lawyer" means

(a) a person admitted to practice law in this jurisdiction;

(b) a person formerly admitted to practice law in this jurisdiction or any other jurisdiction with respect to acts committed prior to resignation, suspension, disbarment or transfer to inactive status, or with respect to acts subsequent thereto that amount to the practice of law;

(c) a person admitted to practice law in another jurisdiction who is specially admitted by a court in this jurisdiction for a particular proceeding;

(d) a person admitted to practice law in another jurisdiction who practices law or renders any legal services in this jurisdiction; and

(e) the assignee of any of the above-named persons in regard to rights or responsibilities related to the fees or costs that are the subject of the arbitration.

(5) "Panel" means the arbitrator(s) assigned to hear a fee dispute and to issue a decision.

(6) "Party" means the client, lawyer(s) responsible for the representation, the lawyer's assignee and any third person or entity who may be liable for payment of, or entitled to a refund of lawyer's fees.

(7) "Petition" means a written request for fee arbitration in a form approved by the Commission.

(8) "Petitioner" means the party requesting fee arbitration.

(9) "Respondent" means the party with whom the petitioner has a fee dispute.

B. Establishment; Purpose. It is the policy of the [highest court of appellate jurisdiction] to encourage the informal resolution of fee disputes between lawyers who practice law in [name of jurisdiction] and their clients. In the event such informal resolution cannot be achieved, The [highest court of appellate jurisdiction] hereby establishes through adoption of these Rules, a program and procedures for the arbitration of disputes concerning any and all fees and/or costs paid, charged, or claimed for professional services by lawyers.

C. Commission Authority. A lawyer admitted to practice in this jurisdiction is subject to the authority of the Fee Arbitration Commission in this jurisdiction, regardless of where the conduct occurs. A lawyer not admitted in this jurisdiction is also subject to the authority of the Fee Arbitration Commission of this jurisdiction if the lawyer provides any legal services related to the matter that is the subject of the arbitration in this jurisdiction.

D. Choice of Law. In any exercise of the authority of the Fee Arbitration Commission of this jurisdiction, the rules of professional conduct to be applied shall be as follows:

(1) for conduct in connection with a matter pending before a tribunal, the rules of the tribunal shall apply; and

(2) for any other conduct, the rules of the jurisdiction in which the conduct occurred, or, if the predominant effect of the conduct is in a different jurisdiction, the rules of that jurisdiction shall be applied to the conduct.

E. Arbitration Mandatory for Lawyers. Fee arbitration pursuant to these Rules is voluntary for clients and mandatory for lawyers if commenced by a client. If at any time the parties have agreed, in writing, to submit fee disputes to Mandatory Fee Arbitration, arbitration is mandatory for both the lawyer and the client.

F. Binding and Nonbinding Arbitration:

(1) Fee Arbitration is only binding if,

(a) all parties have agreed in writing, after the dispute has arisen, that it will be binding;

(b) None of the parties have sought a trial de novo within 30 days after service of the decision. This period shall not be extended by an application for modification of decision as permitted under Rule 6(C).

(2) A party who is found to have willfully failed to appear for the arbitration hearing is not entitled to a *trial de novo*. The determination of whether the party's non-appearance at hearing was willful shall be made by the court determining a motion for *trial de novo*. The arbitrator's finding on the issue of willful non-appearance is admissible in the court proceeding.

(3) after all parties have agreed in writing to be bound by an arbitration decision in accordance with Rule 1(F)(1), a party may not withdraw from that agreement unless all parties agree to the withdrawal in writing. At any time during the proceedings, the parties may agree in writing to be bound by the decision.

G. Disputes Covered. Disputes concerning fees, costs, or both paid, charged, or claimed for professional services by a lawyer are subject to these Rules except:

(1) disputes where the lawyer is also admitted to practice in another jurisdiction, the lawyer maintains no office in this jurisdiction, and no material portion of the legal services was rendered this jurisdiction

(2) claims for affirmative relief for damages against the lawyer based upon alleged malpractice or professional misconduct except as provided in Rule 5(T);

(3) disputes where entitlement to and the amount of the fees and/or costs charged, claimed or paid to a lawyer by the client or on the client's behalf have been authorized by statute or are determinable by court order, and;

(4) disputes where the request for arbitration is filed more than [four] year(s) after the client-lawyer relationship has been terminated or more than [four] year(s) after the final billing has been received by the client, whichever is later, unless a civil action concerning the disputed amount is not barred by the statute of limitations.

H. Notice of Right to Arbitration; Stay of Proceedings; Waiver by Client:

(1) **Prior to or at the time of service of a summons in a civil action against his or her client for the recovery of fees, costs, or both for professional services rendered, a lawyer shall deliver to the client or the person liable for payment of the lawyer's fees if other than the client a written notice of the client's right to arbitrate under the fee arbitration program. The notice, in a form approved by the Commission, shall include a provision advising the client that failure to file a Petition for Fee Arbitration within 30 days of receipt of notice of the right to arbitrate shall constitute a waiver of the right to arbitrate. Failure to give this notice shall be grounds for dismissal of the civil action without prejudice;**

(2) if a lawyer commences a fee collection action in any court or other tribunal, the lawyer must notify the court or other appropriate authority r that a Petition for Arbitration was filed with the Commission within [thirty] days of service of the notice of the right to arbitrate;

(3) after a client files a timely Petition, the lawyer shall refrain from any judicial or non-judicial collection activities related to the fees and/or costs in dispute pending the outcome of the arbitration; and

(4) unless all parties agree in writing to the arbitration, the right of the client to petition or an arbitration is waived if:
   a) the client fails to file a Petition for Arbitration within [thirty] days of service of the notice of right to arbitrate or
   b) the client commences or maintains an action or files any pleading seeking judicial resolution of the fee dispute, or seeks affirmative relief against the lawyer for damages based upon alleged malpractice or professional misconduct
   c) the client files an answer or equivalent response in an action or other proceeding prior to filing a petition for fee arbitration, if notice of the client's right to fee arbitration was properly given pursuant to this Rule, unless the client can show good cause for filing the answer or equivalent response after receiving notice of the right to arbitration.

Comment

[1] A fee arbitration system provides lawyers and clients with an out of-court method of resolving disputes regarding lawyer's fees, costs, or both that is expeditious, confidential, inexpensive, and impartial. The court should ensure adequate funding for an effective program.

[2] For the purpose of these Rules, "assignee" refers to a person to whom the lawyer has transferred any interest in or right to the fees or costs that are the subject of the arbitration.

[3] The scope of these rules includes costs charged by the lawyer as well as fees because in many cases, fees and costs are inextricably linked. The fee arbitration process should be able to resolve both issues in one process.

[4] A client who believes he or she may have been overcharged by a lawyer may have the lawyer's fee reviewed without incurring the expense of formal litigation. Participation in the Fee Arbitration Program is mandatory for lawyers if the request for arbitration is commenced by a client. Because the inherent regulatory authority of the highest court of appellate jurisdiction extends only to lawyers, fee arbitration is not mandatory for clients unless agreed to pursuant to these Rules. If the parties agreed, in writing, to submit their disputes over fees and costs to the Fee Arbitration Program, then arbitration is also mandatory for the client. The parties may enter into such an agreement at any time.

[5] The fee arbitration decision is binding only upon written agreement of the parties entered into after the fee dispute has arisen. While the lawyer and client may agree to enter into fee arbitration to settle a potential fee dispute before a dispute arises, the client should not be asked to surrender the right to challenge the fee arbitration decision before the dispute arises. This distinction acknowledges the fact that a client's considerations at the onset of the client-lawyer relationship may change if the relationship becomes adversarial. In the absence of a written agreement to be bound by the arbitration decision, any party may seek a trial de novo within 30 days after service of the decision. If the parties have an existing private arbitration agreement to resolve the fee dispute outside of the Fee Arbitration Program, then private arbitration would substitute for a trial de novo The decision becomes binding if neither party seeks a trial de novo within the 30-day period. However, a party who is found to have willfully failed to appear for the arbitration hearing is not entitled to a trial de novo following nonbinding arbitration.

[6] An alternative approach, which currently works effectively in those jurisdictions where it has been adopted, is to provide for arbitration that is both mandatory and binding in all cases. Under such a system, the arbitration decision is binding on the parties subject to appeal only in cases of demonstrable and fundamental unfairness in the procedures utilized in deciding the matter.

[7] A lawyer must notify a client of the right to participate in Fee Arbitration Program prior to or at the time of service of a summons in a civil action against the client to recover fee and/or costs for professional services. Notice is accomplished by delivery, to the client, in accordance with Rule 10(A), of the Notice form approved by the Commission The client must file a Petition for Fee Arbitration within [thirty] days of receipt of service of such notice or the client waives the right to petition or maintain an arbitration proceeding under these rules. If all parties agree to set aside any purported waiver, the fee arbitration can proceed even if the client did not file the Petition for Fee Arbitration within the [thirty] day period.

[8] A third person who is not the client, but who the lawyer believes is liable for or who claims an entitlement to a refund of lawyer's fees or costs, is entitled to receive notice of the right to arbitration and to appear as a party in fee arbitration. Fee arbitration between a lawyer and a non-client is not intended to abrogate the requirement that the lawyer exercise independence of professional judgment on behalf of the client. Absent the client's written consent to disclosure of confidential information, a fee arbitration is not intended to abrogate the lawyer's duty to maintain the confidentiality of information relating to the representation of the client, unless such disclosure is otherwise permitted by law, applicable rules, or court order. Absent the client's signature on the request for arbitration, when an arbitration with a non-client is initiated, notice of the request should be sent to the client at the client's last known address.

[9] If the parties have not entered into a written fee agreement that provides for fee arbitration , the client may also waive the right to the fee arbitration program by commencing a civil action, filing any pleading seeking judicial resolution of the fee dispute, or seeking affirmative relief against the lawyer for damages based on alleged malpractice, or by filing an answer to a civil action or equivalent pleading after having received notice of the client's right to arbitration from the lawyer, unless the client can show good cause why the answer was filed after receiving notice of the right to fee arbitration. This provision assumes that notice was properly

given. Waiving the right to the fee arbitration program in these limited circumstances prevents the same facts from being the subject matter of the arbitration and a civil action and discourages forum shopping. Nothing herein precludes a client from filing a complaint with the disciplinary authority. Nothing in these Rules prevents the filing of a malpractice action after a decision is rendered in the fee arbitration proceeding if the malpractice action is otherwise permitted under the applicable statute of limitations. In accordance with Rule 7.B.(4), a decision under these rules is not admissible in a subsequent malpractice action or trial de novo following nonbinding arbitration except as provided in these Rules.

[10] The Fee Arbitration Program can be expanded by the Commission with applicable rules to arbitrate fee disputes between lawyers provided the petitioning lawyer gives notice to the client and the client joins the request for arbitration as a party.

[11] The Commission is not authorized to impose or require an automatic stay of any civil action or other judicial or administrative proceeding. It is the responsibility of the lawyer who commenced an action or other proceeding to collect fees to notify the court or program administering the other proceeding that a timely request for arbitration was filed. The lawyer should also agree to refrain from judicial or non-judicial collection pending the outcome of the fee arbitration.

Rule 2. Fee Arbitration Commission

A. Appointment of Commission. The [highest court of appellate jurisdiction] shall appoint a Fee Arbitration Commission to administer the Fee Arbitration Program. The [highest court of appellate jurisdiction] shall designate one member to serve as Chair of the Commission.

B. Composition. The Commission shall consist of [nine] members of whom one-third shall be nonlawyers. Members shall be appointed for terms of three years or until a successor has been appointed. Appointments shall be on a staggered basis so that the number of terms expiring shall be approximately the same each year. No members shall be appointed for more than two consecutive full terms, but members appointed for less than a

full term (either originally or to fill a vacancy) may serve two full terms in addition to such part of a term.

C. Duties of the Commission. The Commission shall have the following powers and duties:

(1) to appoint, remove and provide appropriate training for lawyer and nonlawyer arbitrators and arbitration panels;

(2) to interpret these rules;

(3) to approve forms and decide form language;

(4) to establish written procedures that afford a full and equal opportunity to all parties to present relevant evidence;

(5) to issue an annual report and periodic policy recommendations, as needed, to the [highest court of appellate jurisdiction] regarding the program;

(6) to maintain all records of the Fee Arbitration Program;

(7) to determine challenges for cause where an arbitrator has not voluntarily acceded to a challenge;

(8) to determine challenges to the Fee Arbitration Program's jurisdiction to arbitrate a dispute, including claims that the client has waived the right to arbitration or that the dispute is not subject to the Fee Arbitration Program;

(9) to educate the public and the bar about the Fee Arbitration Program; and

(10) to perform all acts necessary for the effective operation of the Fee Arbitration Program.

Comment

[1] Overall authority to administer the Fee Arbitration Program is delegated by the highest court of appellate jurisdiction to the Commission. Both lawyers and nonlawyers serve on the Commission. Commission members are appointed by the court for a three year term. The court should ensure diversity in the membership of the Commission.

[2] Members may be appointed for a period not to exceed two consecutive full terms and a portion of an additional term, if appointed originally to less than a full term. A rotation system is employed in the appointment of members so that, generally, the terms of one-third of the members expire annually. This procedure preserves continuity while inviting the fresh ideas that new personnel inevitably bring to a task.

[3] The Commission has the duty to inform the bar and the public about the Fee Arbitration Program through such means as brochures, public service announcements, and any other means available. There should be a central place where the public can call with questions about lawyers and which can refer appropriate matters to the Fee Arbitration Program. Members of the bar should be encouraged to inform any member of the public known to have a fee dispute with a lawyer about the right to seek fee arbitration or to pursue other available means to resolve the dispute, such as mediation.

[4] Depending on funding, pro bono requirements, and other considerations, the Commission may authorize the reimbursement of reasonable costs and expenses to its members and to arbitrators. The Commission may employ staff to perform functions delegated by the Commission. The Commission can authorize local bar associations to sponsor and conduct fee arbitration programs. However, a client who believes he or she may not be able to obtain a fair resolution at the local level should be permitted to utilize the statewide program.

Rule 3. Arbitrators

A. List of Approved Arbitrators. The Commission shall maintain a list of approved arbitrators and shall adopt written standards for the appointment of the arbitrators. Such standards should ensure appropriate training and experience for arbitrators as well as diversity in the background and experience of the arbitrators. Arbitrators shall be appointed for terms of [three] years and may be reappointed. For good cause, the Commission may remove an arbitrator from the list of approved arbitrators and may appoint a replacement member to serve the balance of the term of the removed member.

B. Panels. The Commission shall appoint panels from the list of approved arbitrators. For disputes involving [$7,500] or more, the panel shall consist of three arbitrators of whom one shall be a nonlawyer member. For disputes involving less than [$7,500], or in any case if the parties so stipulate, the panel shall consist of a sole arbitrator who shall be a lawyer. If the panel consists of three members, the Commission shall designate one lawyer member to act as Chair of the panel and to preside at the

arbitration hearing. When a three-member panel is appointed, all panel members must be present for the panel to proceed, except, the parties may agree, in writing, to accept a single lawyer arbitrator in lieu of a three member panel.

C. Area of Practice. At the option of the client, one member of a three-member panel or the sole arbitrator shall be a lawyer with significant experience in the same area of law as the underlying matter that gave rise to the dispute. The client shall be informed of this option (as part of the notice of the right to arbitration).

D. Impartiality. Within [five] days of the notification of appointment to a panel, an arbitrator shall notify the Commission of any. reason why the arbitrator's impartiality might reasonably be questioned, including, but not limited to the circumstances listed in ABA Model Code of Judicial Conduct Rule 2.11(A). Upon notification of the conflict, the Commission shall appoint a replacement from the list of approved arbitrators.

E. Challenges. Each party may disqualify one arbitrator without cause and may challenge any arbitrator for cause. A challenge for cause must include the reason for the challenge. Any challenge or request for disqualification shall be filed within [fifteen] days after service of the notice of appointment. If the challenge or request for disqualification is not timely filed, it will be ineffective, unless good cause is shown why the request was not timely filed An arbitrator shall accede to a reasonable challenge and the Commission shall appoint a replacement. If an arbitrator does not voluntarily accede, the Commission shall decide whether to appoint a replacement. The decision of the Commission on challenges shall be final.

F. Prohibited Contact with Arbitrators. A party or a lawyer or representative acting for a party shall not directly or indirectly communicate with an arbitrator regarding a matter pending before such arbitrator, except:

(1) at scheduled hearings;

(2) in writing with a copy to all other parties, or their representative counsel, if any, and the Commission;

(3) for the sole purpose of scheduling a hearing date or other administrative procedure with notice of same to other parties;

(4) for the purpose of obtaining the issuance of a subpoena as set forth in these Rules; or

(5) in the event of an emergency.

G. Duties. The panel shall have the following powers and duties:

(1) to take and hear evidence pertaining to the proceeding;

(2) to administer oaths and affirmations;

(3) to compel, by subpoena, the attendance of witnesses and the production of books, papers, and documents pertaining to the proceeding,

(4) to consider challenges to the validity of subpoenas;

(5) to issue decisions; and

(6) to perform all acts necessary to conduct an effective arbitration hearing.

Comment

[1] The Commission appoints both lawyers and nonlawyers to serve as arbitrators for [three] year renewable terms, and maintains a list of approved arbitrators. An arbitration panel composed of lawyers and nonlawyers results in a more balanced evaluation of fee disputes and enhances the credibility of the fee arbitration program for clients. When a Petition is received, the Commission appoints from the list of approved arbitrators a panel of one or three arbitrators to hear the matter, depending on the amount in dispute. The Commission may hire staff or designate a presiding arbitrator to handle the appointment of panels or other administrative tasks as delegated by the Commission. The number of people on the list of approved arbitrators should not be so large as to prevent the participating arbitrators from obtaining sufficient experience in the program.

[2] Appointments to the list of approved arbitrators should represent all segments of the profession and the general population, including diversity on the basis of race, gender and practice setting. Arbitrators should also be dispersed throughout the state to increase access to the fee arbitration process.

[3] The Commission should adopt written standards for appointment of arbitrators which may include compliance with training requirements, ability to meet minimum time and case commitments, years in practice and experience. Standards should exclude disbarred or suspended lawyers, and lawyers with prior criminal convictions that reflect adversely on the lawyer's honesty, trustworthiness or fitness as a lawyer in other respects. All panels of more than one arbitrator should include one nonlawyer member.

[4] Members of panels exercise a quasi-judicial role and should, therefore, be disqualified upon the same grounds and conditions applicable to judges. The Commission should provide that within [fifteen] days after service of the notice of appointment, any party may file one peremptory challenge. In the event of a peremptory challenge, the Commission should relieve the challenged arbitrator and appoint a replacement.

[5] Panels do not render advisory opinions but, rather, adjudicate fee controversies between lawyers and clients.

[6] In jurisdictions with a high volume of arbitration cases, consideration should be given to having pre-set arbitration panels that meet at specified times to simplify the scheduling of hearings.

Rule 4. Commencement of Proceedings

A. Petition to Arbitrate. A fee arbitration proceeding shall commence with the filing of a Petition for Arbitration on a form approved by the Commission and paying the appropriate filing fee as established by the {highest court of appellate jurisdiction}. Any person who is not the client of the lawyer but who has paid or may be liable for the lawyer's fees may commence or join the arbitration as a party to the arbitration. The Petition for Arbitration must be signed by the client and/or any other proper party seeking fee arbitration.

B. Commission Review. The Commission shall review the Petition to determine if it is properly completed and if the Commission has jurisdiction. If the Petition is not properly completed, the Commission will return it to the petitioner and specify what clarification or additional information is required. If the Commission believes, based on the face of the Petition, that the fee arbitration program does not have jurisdiction, the petitioner shall be so advised. The parties shall be given an opportunity to submit written statements supporting their respective positions. The Commission will make a determination of whether jurisdiction should be accepted based on these Rules and the written materials submitted.

C. Service of Petition; Response. Within [five] days of the receipt of a properly completed Petition, the Commission shall serve a copy of the Petition, along with a Fee Arbitration Response Form on

the respondent, and provide notice to the law firm, if any, with which a lawyer-party is associated that a petition for arbitration has been filed. Within [twenty] days after service, the respondent shall file the completed Fee Arbitration Response Form with the Commission which shall forward a copy to all other parties. If the respondent is a lawyer, the respondent shall set forth in the response the name of any other lawyer or law firm who the lawyer claims is responsible for all or part of the client's claim. Within [five] days of receipt of the response, the Commission shall serve on the lawyer(s) named in the Response a copy of the Petition for Arbitration and a Fee Arbitration Response Form for completion, with a copy to the law firm, if any, with which a lawyer-party is associated. Within [twenty] days after service, the lawyer(s) may file the completed Fee Arbitration Response Form with the Commission which shall forward a copy to all other parties.

D. Failure of a Lawyer Respondent to Respond. Failure of a lawyer respondent to file the Fee Arbitration Response Form shall not delay the scheduling of a hearing; however, in any such case the panel may, in its discretion, refuse to consider evidence offered by the lawyer that would reasonably be expected to have been disclosed in the response.

E. Client Consent Required. If a lawyer files a Petition for Arbitration, the arbitration shall proceed only if the client files a written consent within [thirty] days of service of the Petition.

F. Settlement of Disputes. If the dispute giving rise to the Petition for Arbitration has been settled, upon reasonable confirmation of that settlement, the matter shall be dismissed by the Commission or by the panel if one has been assigned.

G. Appointment of Panel. The Commission shall, within [ten] days after receipt of the Petition for Arbitration, appoint a panel and mail to the parties written notification of the name(s) of the panel member(s) assigned to hear the matter.

Comment

[1] The fee arbitration process begins with the filing of a Petition for Arbitration on a form approved by the Commission. The respondent has twenty days after service to return the Fee Arbitration Response Form. The process is commenced either unilaterally by a client or by the lawyer with

the client's consent. If it is initiated by the client, participation is mandatory on the part of the lawyer.

[2] The Fee Arbitration Program is designed to be simple and fast. Consequently, most cases should be concluded within six months.

[3] The respondent lawyer(s) named by the client as being the person(s) responsible for refunding an unearned fee is entitled to identify another lawyer(s) as being responsible for providing such refund to the client. The client must be notified that another lawyer(s) has been so named and that the client has the right to join that named individual in the fee arbitration.

[4] Nothing in these Rules precludes a client from naming more than one lawyer in a fee arbitration if each named lawyer has either had direct or actual responsibility for the underlying representation or is named as the billing lawyer for the underlying representation.

[5] If a respondent lawyer fails to timely file a Fee Arbitration Response Form, the hearing will nonetheless be held in the normal course and the panel may, in its discretion, refuse to consider evidence offered by the respondent lawyer that would reasonably be expected to have been disclosed in the Response. This is not intended as a default procedure. It will still be necessary for the panel to assess the evidence presented and issue a decision.

[6] The Commission must serve a copy of the Petition and the Fee Response Form on the law firm, if any, of which a lawyer is a member. The purpose of this rule is to assure that where a law firm is due a fee, or is obligated therefor, the law firm will have notice of the arbitration and an opportunity to participate. Notice of the fee arbitration proceeding also allows the associated law firm the opportunity to identity and address problematic billing patterns in a timelier manner.

Rule 5. Hearing

A. Notice of Hearing. The panel shall set the date, time and place for the hearing. The panel shall send written notice of the hearing to the parties not less than [thirty] but no more than [sixty] days in advance of the hearing date, unless otherwise agreed by the parties.

B. Representation by Counsel. Any party, at their expense, may be represented by counsel.

C. Recording of Proceedings. No stenographic, audio, or video recording of the hearing is permissible.

D. Continuances. For good cause shown, a panel may continue a hearing upon the request of a party or upon the panel's own motion.

E. Oaths and Affirmations. The testimony of witnesses shall be by oath or affirmation administered by the sole arbitrator or panel Chair.

F. Panel Quorums. All three arbitrators shall be required for a quorum where the panel consists of three members. A panel of three arbitrators shall act with the concurrence of at least two arbitrators. Any dissenting positions must be filed with the majority decision.

G. Appearance; Failure of a Party to Appear. Appearance by a party at a scheduled hearing shall constitute waiver by said party of any deficiency with respect to the giving of notice of hearing. The panel shall proceed in the absence of any party or representative who, after due notice, fails either to be present or to obtain a continuance. A decision shall be made on the basis of the petition, response, testimony of the party in attendance and other materials presented, and not based on the default of a party. The panel shall require parties who are present to submit such evidence as the panel may require to issue a decision. A decision may be made in favor of a party who is absent if the evidence so warrants. If neither party appears, the panel will issue a decision based on the petition, response, and other materials presented prior to the arbitration.

H. Waiver of Personal Appearance. Any party may waive personal appearance and designate a lawyer or nonlawyer representative to appear at the hearing to submit the client's written testimony and exhibits with the client's written declaration under oath to the panel. Such declarations shall be filed with the panel at least [ten] days prior to the hearing. If all parties, in writing, waive appearances at a hearing, the matter may be decided on the basis of written submissions. If the panel concludes that oral presentations are necessary, the panel may schedule a hearing.

I. Telephonic Hearings. In its discretion, a panel may permit a party to appear or present witness testimony at the hearing by telephonic conference call.

J. **Stipulations.** Agreements between the parties as to issues not in dispute and the voluntary exchange of documents prior to the hearing are encouraged.

K. **Evidence.** The panel shall accept such evidence as is relevant and material to the dispute and request additional evidence as necessary to understand and resolve the dispute. The rules of evidence [of the jurisdiction] need not be strictly followed. The parties shall be entitled to be heard, to present evidence and to cross-examine parties and witnesses. The panel shall judge the relevance and materiality of the evidence.

L. **Subpoenas.** Upon request of a party the panel shall issue in blank subpoenas for witnesses or documents necessary to a resolution of the dispute. The requesting party shall be responsible for service of the subpoenas.

M. **Reopening of Hearing.** For good cause shown, the panel may reopen the hearing at any time before a decision is issued.

N. **Death or Incompetency of a Party.** In the event of death or incompetency of a party, the personal representative of the deceased party or the guardian or conservator of the incompetent may be substituted.

O. **Burden of Proof.** The burden of proof shall be on the lawyer to prove the reasonableness of the fee by a preponderance of the evidence.

P. **Order of Proof.** The parties shall present their proof in a manner determined by the panel.

Q. The Commission shall not lose jurisdiction, nor shall any arbitration be dismissed or any decision invalidated or modified in any way, solely because of the Commission's or panel's failure to comply with time requirements set forth in these Rules

R. Upon request, the panel may permit the client to be accompanied by a person for personal assistance or support. Any such person shall be subject to the confidentiality of the arbitration proceeding

S. No discovery is allowable except as specifically set forth in these Rules.

T. Evidence relating to claims of malpractice and final orders of professional misconduct shall be admissible only to the extent that those claims bear upon the fees, costs, or both, to which

the lawyer claims to be entitled. The arbitrators shall not award affirmative relief, in the form of damages or offset or otherwise, for injuries underlying any such claim. Nothing in these Rules shall be construed to prevent the arbitrators from awarding the client a refund of unearned fees, costs, or both previously paid to lawyer.

Comment

[1] The goal of these rules is to provide a setting for hearings that is informal yet fair. To that end, the panel has discretion to grant postponements but need not permit the process to be subverted by unexcused absences. The panel will receive the evidence and testimony offered and judge its relevance and materiality. While the hearing may be conducted informally, witnesses should be required to testify under oath Support persons are permitted to provide support or assistance to the client.

[2] Clients may be hesitant to participate in the fee arbitration program or pursue other civil remedies to settle a fee dispute for fear that confidential information may be disclosed by the lawyer as permitted under Rule 1.6 of the *Model Rules of Professional Conduct*. The prohibition against recordings in fee arbitration proceedings helps to ensure that any disclosure of the client's confidential information is limited to the fee arbitration proceedings.

[3] There is no provision for formal discovery; however, the panel has the power of subpoena, subject to rules of relevancy and materiality.

[4] The burden of proof in fee arbitration is on the lawyer to prove the reasonableness of the fee by a preponderance of the evidence. See ABA *Model Rules of Professional Conduct* Rule 1.5 should admit evidence relating to claims of malpractice and professional misconduct, but only to the extent that those claims bear upon the fees, costs, or both to which the lawyer claims to be entitled. The panel may not award affirmative relief in the form of damages for injuries underlying any such claim.

Rule 6. Decision

A. Form of Decision. The panel's decision shall be in writing and shall include the names of the responsible lawyer(s), a clear statement of the amount in dispute, all questions submitted to the panel, whether and to whom monies are due, and a brief

explanation of the decision. The panel shall be authorized to include an allocation of the filing fee in the arbitration decision; however, it shall not include and award for any other costs of the arbitration, including lawyer's fees resulting from the arbitration proceedings, notwithstanding any contract between the parties providing for such an award of costs or lawyer's fees

B. Issuance of Decision. The decision should be rendered within [thirty] days of the close of the hearing or from the end of any time period permitted by the panel for the filing of supplemental briefs or other materials. No decision is final or is to be served until the decision is approved for procedural compliance by the Commission or its designee. The arbitrator or panel chair shall forward the decision to the Commission which shall serve a copy of the decision on each party to the arbitration. At the time of service of the decision on the parties, the parties shall also be provided with notice of post-arbitration rights, on a form approved by the Commission

C. Modification of Decision:

(1) On application to the panel by a party to a fee dispute, the panel may modify or correct a decision if:

(a) there was an error in the computation of figures or a mistake in the description of a person, thing, or property referred to in the decision;

(b) the decision is imperfect in a matter of form not affecting the merits of the proceeding; or

(c) the decision needs clarification.

(2) Any party may file an application for modification with the panel within [twenty] days after service of the decision and shall serve a copy of the application on all other parties. An objection to the application must be filed with the panel within [ten] days after service of the application for modification.

(3) An application for modification shall not extend the 30-day time period to seek trial de novo under these rules.

(4) Any corrected or amended decision shall be served by the Commission. The time for filing a petition to correct, amend, or vacate the decision begins from the date of service of the amended or corrected decision or the date of

denial of the request for correction or amendment of the decision

D. Retention of Files. The Commission shall maintain all fee arbitration files for a period of [three] years from the date a decision is issued.

Comment

[1] In order to bring a final and speedy conclusion to fee disputes, the decision of the panel is required to be in writing and should be rendered within thirty days. Discretion to extend the time period for unusually complicated or difficult matters should be provided.

[2] Where the petitioner has paid a filing fee for fee arbitration, the arbitrator(s) may allocate the filing fee between both parties. Contracts between the parties providing for lawyer's fees and costs should not be enforced as part of the fee arbitration decision.

[3] The decision should be accompanied by a notice on a form approved by the Commission advising the parties of their rights to judicial relief subsequent to the arbitration proceeding

Rule 7. Effect of Decision; Enforcement

A. Compliance with Decision.

(1) Where the parties have agreed to be bound by the arbitration or have settled the dispute, the parties shall have [thirty] days from service of the written decision or the date the stipulation of settlement is signed by the parties to comply with the decision or settlement.

(2) Where there is no agreement to be bound by the arbitration, any party is entitled to a trial de novo if sought within thirty days from service of the written decision, except that if a party willfully fails to appear at the arbitration hearing, that party shall not be entitled to a trial de novo. The determination of willfulness shall be made by the court. The party who failed to appear at the arbitration shall have the burden of proving that the failure to appear was not willful. In making its determination, the court may consider any findings made by the arbitrators on the subject of a party's failure to appear. If a trial de novo is not sought within 30 days, the decision becomes binding.

B. Trial De Novo.

(1) If there is an action pending, the trial de novo shall be initiated by filing a rejection of arbitration decision and request for trial in that action within 30 days from service of the written decision.

(2) If no action is pending, the trial de novo shall be initiated by the commencement of an action in the court having jurisdiction over the amount in controversy within thirty days from the service of the written decision.

(3) The party seeking a trial de novo shall be the prevailing party if that party obtains a judgment more favorable than that provided by the arbitration decision, and in all other cases the other party shall be the prevailing party. The prevailing party may, in the discretion of the court, be entitled to an allowance for reasonable attorney's fees and costs incurred in the trial de novo, which allowance shall be fixed by the court. In determining the lawyer's fees, the court shall consider the decision and determinations of the arbitrators, in addition to any other relevant evidence.

(4) Except as provided in this rule, the decision and determinations of the arbitrators shall not be admissible in any action or proceeding and shall not operate as collateral estoppel or res judicata.

C. Petition to Confirm, Correct, or Vacate the Decision.

(1) If a civil action has been stayed pursuant to these rules, any petition to confirm, correct, or vacate the decision shall be filed with the court in which the action is pending, and shall be served in accordance with the [jurisdiction's statutes or rules of civil procedure.]

(2) If no action is pending in any court, the decision may be confirmed, corrected, or vacated by petition to the court having jurisdiction over the amount of the decision, in accordance with the [jurisdiction's statutes or rules of civil procedure.]

(3) A court confirming, correcting or vacating a decision under these rules may award to the prevailing party reasonable fees and costs including, if applicable, fees or costs on appeal, incurred in obtaining confirmation, correction or

vacation of the decision. The party obtaining judgment confirming, correcting, or vacating the decision shall be the prevailing party except that, without regard or consideration of who the prevailing party may be, if a party did not appear at the arbitration hearing in the matter provided by these rules, that party shall not be entitled to attorney's fees or costs upon confirmation, correction, or vacation of the decision. In determining the lawyer's fees, the court shall consider the fee arbitration decision and determination of the arbitrator(s) in addition to any other relevant evidence.

Comment

[1] Thirty days is considered a reasonable time period in which to expect the parties to comply with the decision. The thirty days begins to run when the decision in the fee arbitration process is served on the parties or when a settlement agreement is signed.

[2] The Commission itself has no authority to enforce a decision. Either party may use the summary action mechanisms that are provided by the jurisdiction to obtain a judgment consistent with the panel's decision as expeditiously as possible.

[3] Reasonable fees and costs may be awarded to the prevailing party in an action to confirm, correct or vacate a panel decision, unless the prevailing party failed to appear at the arbitration hearing in the manner provided in the rules. This exception should encourage full participation of the parties in the arbitration proceeding.

[4] Every jurisdiction is encouraged to consider developing means of assisting clients in enforcing decisions. Some jurisdictions use a panel of pro bono lawyers to assist the clients in obtaining civil judgments. Some jurisdictions refer lawyers who fail to comply with a decision or judgment to an appropriate agency for administrative, non-disciplinary action such as that used in the jurisdiction for failure to comply with mandatory continuing legal education requirements or failure to pay registration fees.

Rule 8. Confidentiality

A. Confidentiality of Proceedings. Except as may be otherwise necessary for compliance with these rules or to take ancillary

legal action with respect thereto, all records, documents, files, proceedings and hearings pertaining to the arbitration of any dispute under these rules shall be confidential and will be closed to the public, unless ordered open by a [court of general jurisdiction] upon good cause shown, except that a summary of the facts, without reference to the parties by name, may be publicized in all cases once the proceeding has been formally closed.

B. Confidentiality of Information. A lawyer may reveal information relating to the representation of the client to the extent necessary to establish his or her fee claim. In no event shall such disclosure be deemed a waiver of the confidential character of such information for any other purpose.

C. Confidentiality and Non-Clients. A fee arbitration between a lawyer and a non-client does not limit the lawyer's duty to exercise independence of professional judgment on behalf of the client.

Comment

[1] Rule 8.B is consistent with Rule 1.6(b)(5) of theABA Model Rule of Professional Conduct which permits limited disclosure of otherwise confidential information "to the extent the lawyer reasonably believes necessary to establish a claim or defense . . . in a controversy between the lawyer and the client. "

[2] Fee arbitration may proceed between a non-client and the lawyer. In arbitrations where the client is neither a party nor a witness and is not present at the arbitration hearing, the lawyer should exercise care to avoid abrogating the lawyer's duty to maintain the confidentiality of information relating to the representation of the client. See also Rule 1, Comment [4].

Rule 9. Immunity

A. Parties and Witnesses. Parties and witnesses shall have such immunity as is applicable in a civil action in the jurisdiction.

B. Commissioners; Arbitrators; Staff. Members of the Commission, panels and staff shall be immune from suit for any conduct in the course and scope of their official duties.

RULE 10. SERVICE

A. Method. Service on any party other than a lawyer shall be by personal delivery, by any person authorized by the Chair of the Commission, or by deposit in the United States mail, postage paid, addressed to the person on whom it is to be served at his or her office or home address as last given to the Commission.

B. Official Address of Lawyer. Service on an individual lawyer shall be at the latest address shown on the official membership records of the [highest court of appellate jurisdiction or state bar association.] Notice to a law firm shall be at the address as shown in the Petition for Arbitration Form unless the law firm designates a lawyer to be responsible for the arbitration, in which case, service shall be at the designee's latest address shown on the official membership records of the [highest court of appellate jurisdiction or state bar association.] The method of service shall be in accordance with section 10.A. above.

C. Service on Represented Parties. If either party is represented by counsel, service shall be on the party as indicated in Rules 10.A. and 10.B., and on the counsel at the latest address shown on the official membership records of the [highest court of appellate jurisdiction or state bar association.]

D. Completion of Service. The service is complete at the time of deposit. The time for performing any act shall commence on the date service is complete and shall not be extended by reason of service by mail.

ABA MODEL RULES FOR MEDIATION OF CLIENT—LAWYER DISPUTES

Adopted by the American Bar Association House of Delegates on August 4, 1998.

Mediation of Client—Lawyer Disputes

American Bar Association
Standing Committee on Client Protection
1997–1998

Advisory Commission on Lawyers' Funds for Client Protection 1997–1998

Center for Professional Responsibility

MODEL RULES FOR MEDIATION OF CLIENT—LAWYER DISPUTES

Preface

On February 4, 1992, the American Bar Association House of Delegates adopted the Report of the Commission on Evaluation of Disciplinary Enforcement (the "McKay Commission"). The Commission was created in February 1989 to conduct a nationwide evaluation of lawyer disciplinary enforcement and to provide a model for responsible regulation of the legal profession into the twenty-first century. Recommendation 3 of the McKay Commission Report called for jurisdictions to expand their systems of lawyer regulation by establishing mechanisms to resolve disputes between clients and lawyers and handle non-disciplinary complaints about lawyers. Mechanisms for fee arbitration, mediation, lawyer practice assistance and lawyer substance abuse counseling were recommended.

In 1996 the Joint Committee on Lawyer Regulation of the ABA Center for Professional Responsibility began drafting model rules for the mediation of complaints against lawyers which alleged lesser misconduct. The Committee reviewed mediation programs and rules from California, Colorado, Missouri, New York and Wisconsin. Additionally, the Committee studied the ABA *Model Rules for Fee Arbitration* that had been adopted in February 1995 by the American Bar Association House of Delegates. In 1997, the task of finalizing the mediation rules was passed to the ABA Standing Committee on Client Protection. In December 1997 the Committee circulated for comment a draft of the Model Rules to Association entities and judicial and legal organizations across the country. On August 4, 1998, at its Annual meeting in Toronto, the American Bar Association House of Delegates adopted the black-letter of the *Model Rules for Mediation of Client-Lawyer Disputes.*

The *Model Rules for Mediation of Client-Lawyer Disputes* are designed to assist jurisdictions interested in implementing a voluntary mediation program. The Model Rules will be subject to modification at the level of local implementation. The Comments do not add obligations to the Model Rules but provide guidance for conducting a mediation program in compliance with the Model Rules.

Mediation is a process by which those who have a dispute, misunderstanding or conflict come together and, with the assistance of a trained neutral mediator, resolve the issues and problems in a way that meets the needs and interests of both parties. Mediation can help to preserve the client-lawyer relationship. For both clients and lawyers, the mediation process is an alternative to litigation or other more formal and expensive dispute resolution mechanisms. The mediation process will benefit the public by directly addressing instances where a lawyer is alleged to have engaged in lesser misconduct but the misconduct does not warrant a formal disciplinary proceeding. The mediation process will also protect the public by removing matters involving lesser misconduct from the disciplinary system and thereby allowing disciplinary counsel to focus their efforts on more serious matters.

Rule 1. General Principles and Jurisdiction

A. Definitions:

(1) a "Client" means a person or entity who directly or through an authorized representative, consults or retains a lawyer in the lawyer's professional capacity.

(2) "Commission" means the Client-Lawyer Mediation Commission.

(3) "Lawyer" means any lawyer admitted to practice law in [name of jurisdiction], including any formerly admitted lawyer, any lawyer specially admitted by a court of this jurisdiction for a particular proceeding and any lawyer not admitted in this jurisdiction who practices law or renders or offers to render any legal services in this jurisdiction.

B. Establishment; Purpose. It is the policy of the [highest court of the jurisdiction] to encourage the informal resolution of disputes between lawyers who practice law in [name of jurisdiction] and their clients. To that end, the [highest court of the jurisdiction] hereby establishes through adoption of these rules, a program for mediation of client-lawyer disputes. The program includes mediations referred by [the lawyer disciplinary agency] and voluntary mediation requests made by the client or by the lawyer, if both the client and the lawyer agree to mediate.

C. Jurisdiction:

(1) any lawyer is subject to these rules for mediation.

(2) the Commission has jurisdiction over disputes that involve lesser misconduct or no misconduct on the part of the lawyer and appear to be resolvable by mediation.

(3) the Commission has jurisdiction over disputes referred by [the lawyer disciplinary agency] and voluntary mediations in which a lawyer or client requests mediation and the other party agrees.

Comment

[1] The mediation program described in these rules is part of this jurisdiction's comprehensive lawyer regulatory system. The comprehensive system includes: [a lawyer discipline and disability system, a client

protection fund, mandatory arbitration of fee disputes, mediation, law office management assistance, and lawyer assistance programs].

[2] Since mediation is a process that works by building consensus and agreement, the mediation process can preserve existing client-lawyer or other fiduciary relationships by allowing both sides to air their grievances and work together on a solution agreeable to all parties. When handled by a skilled mediator, the process can be simple and efficient, saving time and money for both parties. The lawyer's willingness to have a third party assist in resolving the dispute can demonstrate to the client that the lawyer's intention is to act in the client's best interest.

[3] Mediation is not suitable when the dispute involves an allegation of lawyer misconduct, which, if true, would warrant a sanction restricting the lawyer's license to practice law. Mediation is appropriate when the dispute involves no allegation of lawyer misconduct or an allegation of lesser misconduct as defined in [jurisdiction's rules of disciplinary enforcement]. It is appropriate because there is little or no injury to a client, the public, the legal system, or the profession, and there is little likelihood of repetition by the lawyer.

[4] Examples of disputes that might be referred to mediation include allegations of a lawyer's failure or refusal to return a client's file based on a fee dispute with the client, release a lien on a client's recovery in a case in which the lawyer has been succeeded by another lawyer, withdraw from representation upon being discharged by the client, conclude a legal representation by preparing an essential dispositive document, such as the findings of fact and conclusions of law in a divorce or the final account in an estate, return an unearned fee or a portion of the fee, comply with his or her agreement with a medical provider on the client's behalf or communicate concerning the status of a matter.

[5] Other examples of situations in which the parties might agree to voluntary mediation could include allegations of a client's failure to pay or fulfill the contract, pay for costs (including future costs) or communicate with the lawyer.

[6] The primary purpose of the program is to resolve complaints referred from the jurisdiction's lawyer disciplinary agency. Therefore, such referrals should be given priority over voluntary mediations.

[7] Mediation can be used to complement fee arbitration proceedings. The Commission may accept jurisdiction in a dispute in which a fee arbitration proceeding is pending but has not yet begun. The intention is to

solve the dispute in a less formal way, if possible, not to refer complainants back and forth between the two programs.

Rule 2. Mediation Commission

A. Appointment of Commission. The [highest court of the jurisdiction] shall appoint a Mediation Commission to administer the Mediation Program. The [highest court of the jurisdiction] shall designate one member to serve as Chair of the Commission.

B. Composition. The Commission shall consist of [six] members, of whom at least one-third shall be nonlawyers. Members shall be appointed for terms of three years except where a vacancy has occurred in which event appointments shall be for the unexpired portion of the term being filled. Appointments shall be on a staggered basis so that the number of terms expiring shall be approximately the same each year. No members shall be appointed for more than two consecutive full terms, but members appointed for less than a full term (either originally or to fill a vacancy) may serve two full terms in addition to such part of a term.

C. Duties of the Commission. The Commission shall have the following powers and duties to:

(1) appoint and remove mediators and provide appropriate training;

(2) interpret these rules;

(3) establish written procedures not inconsistent with these rules;

(4) issue an annual report and periodic policy recommendations, as needed, to the [highest court of the jurisdiction] regarding the program;

(5) maintain all records of the Mediation Program;

(6) determine challenges for cause where a mediator has not voluntarily acceded to a challenge;

(7) educate the public and the bar about the Mediation Program;

(8) perform all acts necessary for the effective operation of the program; and

(9) establish fee schedules and oversee financial matters.

Comment

[1] Overall authority to administer the Mediation Program is delegated by [the highest court of the jurisdiction] to the Commission. The court should ensure diversity in the membership of the Commission.

[2] The Commission has authority to limit the types of matters accepted for mediation. Personal disputes and business matters where one of the parties is a lawyer but the allegations do not involve the practice of law are not appropriate for mediation under these rules. Mediation of disputes between lawyers is not precluded by these rules where the complaint otherwise meets the guidelines of matters that are appropriate for mediation.

[3] The Commission has the authority to establish reasonable fees for the program and also to waive fees in cases of hardship. No fee should be charged a client if the charging of the fee would unduly restrict the client's access to the mediation process. Additionally, in mediations referred by [the lawyer disciplinary agency], the client should not be charged a fee for participating in the mediation.

[4] With respect to the funding of the mediation program, it is envisioned that there will be minimal costs involved: lawyer and nonlawyer volunteers will be serving as mediators. The Commission may delegate the day-to-day administration of the Mediation Program to staff assigned to the lawyer disciplinary agency. However, a state or local bar association could administer this component of the lawyer regulation system.

RULE 3. MEDIATORS

A. **List of Approved Mediators. The Commission shall maintain a list of approved mediators, both lawyers and nonlawyers, and shall adopt written standards for the appointment of the mediators. Mediators should represent all segments of the profession and the general population, including diversity on the basis of race, gender, and practice setting. Mediators shall be appointed for terms of [three] years and may be reappointed. The Commission may remove a mediator from the list of approved mediators for good cause, and may appoint a replacement member to serve the balance of the term of the removed member.**

B. **Conflicts of Interest. Within [20] days of the notification of appointment as a mediator, and prior to the initiation of the**

mediation, the mediator shall notify the Commission if he or she has previously acted as a mediator in the proceeding or in any other related proceeding or of any conflict of interest with a party to the mediation as defined in the [*Code of Judicial Conduct*] with respect to part-time judges. Upon notification of the conflict, the Commission shall appoint a replacement from the list of approved mediators.

C. Challenges for Cause. If either party has cause to object to participation by a mediator, a substitute shall be appointed by the Commission. A challenge for cause shall be filed within [15] days after service of the notice of appointment. A mediator shall accede to a reasonable challenge and the Commission shall appoint a replacement. If a mediator does not voluntarily accede, the Commission shall decide whether to appoint a replacement. The decision of the Commission on challenges shall be final.

D. Duties. The mediator shall have powers and duties to:

(1) grant extensions of time as deemed appropriate;

(2) reschedule or terminate the mediation if a party fails to appear; and

(3) perform all acts necessary to conduct an effective mediation conference.

Comment

[1] Written standards for the appointment of mediators should ensure appropriate training and experience for mediators as well as diversity in the background and experience of the mediators. Mediators should also be dispersed throughout the jurisdiction to increase access to the mediation process.

[2] Mediators should be required to attend an appropriate training course, as determined by the Commission, which should include training in mediation theory, skills and the applicable provisions of the rules of professional conduct.

[3] Mediators exercise a quasi-judicial role and should, therefore, be disqualified upon the same grounds and conditions applicable to parttime judges. The decisions of the mediators should be free from any appearance of outside influence.

Rule 4. The Process

A. **Commencement of Mediation.**

(1) **Referral from Lawyer Disciplinary Agency. Within [15] calendar days after receipt by the Commission of a mediation referral from [the lawyer disciplinary agency], the Commission shall mail to both the lawyer and the complainant a copy of these rules and an agreement to mediate, together with a notice that shall include the name, address and telephone number of the mediation program and the date on which the referral for mediation was received. If the signed agreement to mediate is not returned to the Commission by both parties within [30] calendar days of mailing, the Commission shall close the file, notify the parties that it is closing the file because one or both parties failed to return the agreement, and inform the [lawyer disciplinary agency] of the identity of the party or parties who did not consent to mediation.**

(2) **Voluntary Mediation. Within [15] calendar days after receipt by the Commission of the approved written application for voluntary mediation of a dispute and a signed agreement to mediate, the Commission shall notify the other party of the request and shall forward to that party an agreement to mediate, together with a copy of these Rules and a copy of the written application. If the signed agreement is not returned to the program by the other party within [30] calendar days of mailing, the Commission shall close the file and notify the requestor that the other party did not consent to mediation.**

B. **Assignment of Mediators. The Commission shall notify the parties of the assignment of a mediator within [15] calendar days after receipt of the fully executed agreement to mediate. The notice shall include the name, address and telephone number of the mediator assigned. The mediator shall be assigned at random from the available pool of qualified individuals. Upon withdrawal or removal of a mediator, the Commission shall notify the parties within [10] calendar days of the name, address and telephone number of a new mediator.**

C. Mediation Hearing Date. Within [15] calendar days after the date of mailing of the notice of the assignment of a mediator, the mediator shall arrange a mediation conference date which shall be scheduled to take place within [30] calendar days after the assignment notice mailing date, unless both parties to the mediation agree to a longer date. The mediator shall promptly notify the parties and the Commission of the place, date and time of the conference.

D. The Conference:

(1) only the parties to the mediation, their lawyers, if any, and the mediator are required to be present during the mediation, but the mediator shall have authority to determine if others may be present at and participate in the mediation.

(2) the mediator shall have the authority to meet separately with the parties.

(3) if all parties and the mediator agree, the mediation may be conducted by telephone. In cases of hardship, the mediation may be conducted by telephone at the discretion of the mediator even if all parties do not agree.

(4) if upon completion of the mediation, the parties have an agreement, the mediator shall reduce the agreement of the parties to writing. The parties shall sign as many originals as there are parties to the mediation. A copy of the signed agreement shall be made for the Commission's records. The mediator shall report to the Commission on the Mediation Summary Report form, which will indicate if the dispute was resolved, was not resolved, or did not proceed because a party did not appear (with an indication of which party did not appear). Such agreement and/or report shall be submitted within [15] calendar days after the conclusion of the mediation.

(5) in the case of any mediation referred from the disciplinary agency, the following materials shall be transmitted to the [lawyer disciplinary agency] at the conclusion of the mediation:

a. a duplicate original of the signed mediation agreement described in Rule 4.D.4 above; and

b. the completed Mediation Summary Report form.

Comment

[1] The overwhelming majority of complaints made against lawyers allege instances of lesser misconduct. Summary dismissal of these complaints is one of the chief sources of public dissatisfaction with the lawyer regulation system. These cases seldom justify the resources needed to conduct formal disciplinary proceedings and should be removed from the disciplinary system and handled administratively.

[2] The mediation program established by these rules is designed to receive cases from a number of sources: the central intake office; the disciplinary agency; other agencies within the lawyer regulation system; the courts; or directly from the parties. Referrals from the disciplinary agency will usually be part of a diversion program or an agreement in lieu of discipline, in which a lawyer agrees to mediate a dispute with the understanding that the disciplinary matter will be dismissed upon successful completion of the mediation. Agreement of both the client and the lawyer is required for a matter to be referred to mediation from the disciplinary agency. Matters that come to the mediation program from the central intake office, other agencies, or directly from the parties are voluntary as described in these rules.

[3] The mediator is authorized to determine the rules by which the mediation will proceed. The mediator should conduct the conference informally. At the outset, the mediator should make clear to the parties that the mediator is serving as a mediator and not a judge. The mediator's role is to facilitate communication and suggest ways of resolving the dispute; the mediator is not to impose a settlement on the parties. The mediator should make every effort to hear all the relevant facts, review all the relevant documents, become familiar with any controlling legal principles and seek to bring about an acceptable compromise between the parties. The mediator should make sure that any proposal offered for resolution of the matter is clearly understood by the parties and perceived to be fair.

Rule 5. Confidentiality

A. Except as provided in Rule 4.D.5 above, and Rule 5.B below, all communications, negotiations or settlement discussions by and between participants and/or mediators in the mediation shall remain confidential. All parties attending a mediation shall sign a written agreement that the proceeding will be confidential.

B. Notwithstanding Rule 5.A above, lawyer mediators have a duty to, and nonlawyer mediators should, report conduct that would be reportable under the applicable rules of professional conduct or other applicable statutes or rules.

Comment

[1] Confidentiality in a mediation hearing is of paramount importance. Nevertheless, the need to report lawyer misconduct takes precedence. Lawyer mediators have a duty to, and nonlawyer mediators should, report conduct that would be reportable under the jurisdiction's applicable rules or statutes. A lawyer having knowledge that another lawyer has committed a violation of the [rules of professional conduct] that raises a substantial question as to that lawyer's honesty, trustworthiness or fitness as a lawyer in other respects, must inform the appropriate professional authority. Nonlawyer mediators should refer to this standard in determining their responsibility to report lawyer misconduct. The fact that mediators have a duty to report lawyer misconduct should not have a chilling effect on those parties who are sincere in availing themselves of the benefits of mediation. All mediators may also be required by the laws in their jurisdiction to report to the appropriate agency evidence of other types of misconduct, i.e., child abuse or criminal conduct, that comes to light during a mediation.

Rule 6. Immunity

Communications to the Commission, mediators, or disciplinary counsel relating to lawyer misconduct or disability and testimony given in the proceedings shall be absolutely privileged, and no lawsuit predicated thereon may be instituted against any client or witness. Members of the Commission, mediators, disciplinary counsel, or any person acting on their behalf, and staff shall be immune from suit for any conduct in the course of their official duties.

Comment

[1] The personnel involved in the mediation process are an integral part of the judicial process and are entitled to the same immunity, which is afforded prosecuting lawyers. Immunity protects the independent

judgment of the mediation personnel and avoids diverting the attention of its personnel as well as its resources toward resisting collateral attack and harassment. A policy of conferring absolute immunity encourages those who have some doubt about a lawyer's conduct to submit the matter to the proper agency, where it may be examined and determined.

GUIDELINES FOR THE ADOPTION OF A DEFINITION OF THE PRACTICE OF LAW

Adopted by the American Bar Association House of Delegates on August 11, 2003.

American Bar Association Task Force on the Model Definition of the Practice of Law 2002–2003

Lish Whitson, *Chair*
Seattle, Washington

John T. Berry
Lansing, Michigan

M. Peter Moser
Baltimore, Maryland

Thomas Grella
Asheville, North Carolina

Linda C. Shely
Scottsdale, Arizona

Dudley Humphrey
Winston-Salem, North Carolina

Robert D. Welden
Seattle, Washington

Alice E. Richmond, *Liaison*
ABA Board of Governors
Boston, Massachusetts

Center for Professional Responsibility

Director
Jeanne P. Gray

Counsel to the Task Force
Art H. Garwin

GUIDELINES FOR THE ADOPTION OF A DEFINITION OF THE PRACTICE OF LAW

A. Every jurisdiction should adopt a definition of the practice of law.

B. Each jurisdiction's definition should include the basic premise that the practice of law is the application of legal principles and judgment to the circumstances or objectives of another person or entity.

C. Each jurisdiction should determine who may provide services that are included within the state's or territory's definition of the practice of law and under what circumstances, based upon the potential harm and benefit to the public. The determination should include consideration of minimum qualifications, competence and accountability.

Comment

INTRODUCTION

[1] On August 11, 2003, the American Bar Association House of Delegates adopted the Report and Recommendation of the Task Force on the Model Definition of the Practice of Law. The Task Force began its work by examining codified and case law definitions of the practice of law from around the country.[1] The Task Force conducted hearings and heard testimony about consumer harm from services that are included within the definition of the practice of law that were, in the instances related, provided by unregulated, incompetent providers, as well as testimony about the need to provide additional access to competent services. The Task Force agreed that a definition of the practice of law is an important step in protecting the public from unqualified service providers, eliminating uncertainty for persons working in law-related areas about the propriety of their conduct and enhancing the availability of services that are included within the definition of the practice of law. Moreover, the Task Force was persuaded by the efforts of Arizona, Washington, the District of Columbia and other jurisdictions that already had adopted definitions that it is possible to create a useful definition of the practice of law.

1. *See* http://www.abanet.org/cpr/model-def/model_def_statutes.pdf.

[2] The Task Force's initial discussion draft definition provided a specific model definition of the practice of law and listed the exceptions and exclusions to the definition that might or might not constitute the practice of law, but would be permitted activity by nonlawyers in either event. Upon further deliberation, the Task Force became convinced that the considerations in defining the practice of law in each jurisdiction required that a procedural framework for jurisdictions to follow be recommended instead. The Task Force also became convinced that the necessary balancing test for determining who should be permitted to provide services that are included within the definition of the practice of law is best done at the state level.[2] This was consistent with the Task Force's charge to "consider anew the need to present a model definition . . . and to aid other jurisdictions that may wish to take action." The Task Force acknowledged that each jurisdiction will weigh the factors provided in

2. Each state has a unique culture, a specific legal and social history, a record of experience with nonlawyer activity and an economic, political and social environment that will affect its judgment about the types and amount of nonlawyer activity likely to enhance access to justice and protect the public. *See* American Bar Association Commission on Nonlawyer Practice, NONLAWYER ACTIVITY IN LAW-RELATED SITUATIONS (August 1995) at 135.

This decision by the Task Force to recommend state-by-state consideration of the issue is not meant to contravene existing ABA policy or to establish new policy in regard to the specifics of a definition of the practice of law, as opposed to the framework for creating a definition. Thus, for example, it is not the purpose of this report or its accompanying recommendation to address the special circumstance in which lawyers and others serve as a mediator, arbitrator or neutral in other types of ADR proceedings. Moreover, it is not the intent of the Task Force to suggest that in providing such services these individuals are engaged in the practice of law. In fact, the Task Force recognizes that most states that have considered this issue specifically have excluded the activities of mediators and arbitrators from their definition of the practice of law. *See, e.g.,* Commentary to Rule 49(b)(2), District of Columbia Court of Appeals Rules ("The Rule is not intended to cover the provision of mediation or alternative dispute resolution ("ADR") services. This intent is expressed in the first sentence of the definition of the "practice of law" which requires the presence of two essential factors: The provision of legal advice or services and a client relationship of trust or reliance. ADR services are not given in circumstances where there is a client relationship of trust or reliance; and it is common practice for providers of ADR services explicitly to advise participants that they are not providing the services of legal counsel."); and Washington State Bar Ass'n, Comm. to Define the Practice of Law, Final Report (July 1999), adopted by Washington State Bar Association Board of Governors, September 1999 ("[P]ersons acting in [the] capacity of [mediator, arbitrator, conciliator or facilitator] are not engaged in the practice of law."); *but cf.* New Jersey. Sup. Ct. Advisory Comm. Prof'l Ethics, Op. No. 676 (April 4, 1994) (holding that when a lawyer serves as a third party neutral, he or she "is acting as a lawyer"); *see generally,* Resolution of the ABA Section of Dispute Resolution dated February 2, 2002 (available at http://www.abanet.org/dispute/resolution2002.pdf).

the framework in a manner that is best suited to resolving the harm/ benefit equation for its citizens.[3]

The Basic Premise of the Definition of the Practice of Law

[3] The Task Force studied examples of broad definitions from around the country.[4] Many of them, in some form or another, include providing legal advice.[5] Some definitions specifically mention representing another in court and/or drafting legal documents.[6]

[4] Inherent in the drafting and selection of legal documents is the provision of legal advice. Inherent in the representation of another before a court is the provision of legal advice. This is the clear starting point for any definition of the practice of law. The Task Force determined that the application of legal principles and judgment to the circumstances or objectives of another person or entity is implicit in the giving of legal advice and thus used that expanded notion as the broad basic premise for creating a definition of the practice of law.[7] That broad premise would then be used in conjunction with the third resolution's guide for how each jurisdiction should determine who may provide services that are included within the jurisdiction's definition of the practice of law.

---

3. *See infra*, III. A. *The Balancing Process*.

4. *See* http://www.abanet.org/cpr/model-def/model_def_statutes.pdf for all the definitions the Task Force reviewed.

5. *See, e.g.*, Alaska Stat. § 08.08.230 (Unlawful Practice) and Alaska State Bar Rule 63 (Unauthorized Practice of Law); Ga. Code Ann. § 15-19-50 (Practice of Law Defined); Ky. Rev. Stat. Ann., Rules of the Supreme Court, SCR 3.020 (Practice of Law Defined); Md. Code Ann., Business Occupations & Professions, § 10-101(h) (Definitions); N.M. Stat. Ann., Rules Governing Legal Assistant Services, Rule 20-102 (B) (Definition of Practice of Law); Rule 11 of the Rules of the Supreme Court of Wyoming Providing for the Organization and Government of the Bar Association and Attorneys at Law of the State of Wyoming.

6. *See, e.g.*, Ala. Code § 34-3-6 (Who may practice as attorneys); La. Rev. Stat. § 37:212 (Practice of Law Defined); Mo. Rev. Stat. § 484.010 (Practice of the law and law business defined); N.C. Gen. Stat. Ann. § 84-2.1 ("Practice of law" defined); R.I. Gen. Laws § 11-27-2 ("Practice of law" defined); Tenn. Code Ann. § 23-3-101 (Definitions).

7. The Task Force received many comments that suggested that its draft definition was overly broad. The broad starting point of the second resolution of its recommendation is exactly that, a starting point.

Who May Engage in the Practice of Law and Under What Circumstances

[5] The chief reason for defining the practice of law and regulating those who perform services within the scope of the definition is to protect the public from harm that may result from the activities of dishonest, unethical and incompetent providers.[8] Once the practice of law is defined, a jurisdiction must determine who may perform services that are included within the definition and under what circumstances. The scope of permissible conduct of persons who may engage in activities that are included within the definition of the practice of law will vary among jurisdictions, dependent upon the harm and benefit to the public and the requisite qualifications, competence, accountability and other requirements thought necessary to engage in those activities. Thus, in order to determine who may provide services that are included within the definition of the practice of law, jurisdictions must have sufficient information available to predict which nonlawyers, and under what circumstances, may provide a great benefit and which may create harm.[9]

[6] The basic assumption of the Task Force was that jurisdictions will apply common sense in defining who may be authorized to provide services that are included within the definition of the practice of law and who does not need to be regulated. For instance, advice given by one neighbor to another regarding zoning issues or a mechanic's comments on warranty coverage is not conduct that needs to be regulated.

The Balancing Process

[7] The Task Force recommended that certain factors be balanced to determine who should be able to provide services and under what circumstances. The process of balancing harm and benefit is not an easy one. There is no simple formula. It requires an exercise of discretion and judgment based on the best available evidence. Each jurisdiction should weigh concerns for public protection and consumer safety, access to justice,

8. Potential for harm is too quickly discounted by those who want to expand the field of who may provide services within the definition of the practice of law and too easily found by those who want to restrict the practice of law to lawyers.

9. *See infra, IV. Implementation*, for a discussion regarding the need for each jurisdiction to conduct a study of potential harm.

preservation of individual choice, judicial economy, maintenance of professional standards, efficient operation of the marketplace, costs of regulation and implementation of public policy.[10]

[8] In particular, each jurisdiction should consider the following factors in determining who should be permitted to practice law and under what circumstances. The Task Force recognized that the balancing process may produce divergent results among jurisdictions.

Minimum Qualifications

[9] In most jurisdictions, the qualifications for admission to the practice of law include graduation from an accredited law school, passage of a bar examination with a testing component on professional responsibility law, and determinations of character and fitness. While several jurisdictions have diverged from the traditional model of institutional education, examination and fitness determination, all mandate qualifications for admission to practice law through varying systems of education, testing, apprenticeship, and lawyer mentoring.[11]

[10] As a member of the legal profession, a lawyer serves the complex role as a representative of clients, an officer of the legal system and a public citizen having special responsibility for the quality of justice.[12] The lawyer's complex role includes special obligations such as client confidentiality, conflicts avoidance, competent performance and professional independence that underscore the need for a comprehensive system of minimum qualifications for admission to the practice of law. The principal objective of the qualification system is to ensure that education, training, examination and fitness criteria are satisfied prior to admission

10. *See* American Bar Association Commission on Nonlawyer Practice, Nonlawyer Activity in Law-Related Situations (August 1995) at 135, 136.

11. 1 Comprehensive Guide to Bar Admission Requirements, 2002 Edition, National Conference of Bar Examiners and American Bar Association Section on Legal Education and Admissions to the Bar: 9 jurisdictions allow applicants to write the bar examinations after law office study or correspondence study; 42 jurisdictions require a J.D., LL.B or LL.M to write the bar examination; 25 jurisdictions require a J.D., LL.B. or LL.M from an ABA-approved law school or else a foreign law degree; 4 jurisdictions require completion of certain courses or skills training during law school for initial admission to the bar; 16 jurisdictions require completion of certain courses or skills training after law school for initial admission to the bar.

12. *See* ABA Model Rules of Professional Conduct Preamble: A Lawyer's Responsibilities (2003).

and licensing. Thereafter, the jurisdiction's regulatory system monitors the ethical conduct and competency of lawyers through an extensive system of professional continuing education, periodic registration, professional conduct rules and professional liability standards, and disciplinary enforcement.

[11] A qualification system also should be established for nonlawyers authorized to provide services within the definition of the practice of law. The harm/benefit determination by the jurisdiction authorizing other service providers should dictate the scope and breadth of the system. In the delicate balance of access to justice and public protection, both factors are fundamental.

[12] Jurisdictions should strive to establish minimum qualifications that promote the delivery of services within a framework of public protection, competence and accountability. The system should provide a continuum that starts with minimal necessary qualifications under certain circumstances and proceeds to qualifications that might rival those required of lawyers if the extensiveness or sophistication of the service merits it.

[13] The experience in several jurisdictions and in federal administrative agencies demonstrates diversity in approach. These qualification systems have spanned the spectrum from self-declaration of competence to formal licensure. Many of the qualification systems include components of minimal training, formal education, disclosure of qualifications and training, testing, registration, accreditation, and certification. The challenge for each jurisdiction in setting minimum qualifications is the balancing of the potential risk of harm, the consumer's level of knowledge, the potential benefits to the public and the costs of regulation.[13]

Competence

[14] The skills needed to provide services that are included within the definition of the practice of law and the potential harm that might

13. *See, e.g.*, Md. Code Ann., State Government, § 9-1607.1 (1994) (in-state organizations train and certify tenant advocates to appear against landlords' agents); Wash. Court Rules, Admission to Practice Rule 12 (Limited Practice Rule for Closing Officers); Ariz. Code of Judicial Administration § 7-208 (Legal Document Preparer); ABA Model Guidelines for the Utilization of Legal Assistant Services; Minn. Stat. Ann. § 572.37, Minn. Civil Mediation Act (mediation service providers must provide potential parties with a written statement of qualifications, education, and training before commencing mediation).

result from the lack of competence are primary concerns. The existence of a licensing procedure, whether related to the law license or some other relevant license, is one consideration of this factor. The requirements for a license to practice law demand a prescribed level of competence by those obtaining the license. This usually includes extensive educational and testing requirements to establish competence to practice law.

[15] While the training that lawyers receive in law school prepares them to think analytically in a way that can be applied to any area of practice, many lawyers concentrate their practices in certain areas of the law. Accordingly, there may be areas of the law with which a particular lawyer is not familiar. While the Comment to Model Rule of Professional Conduct 1.1 states that "[a] lawyer can provide adequate representation in a wholly novel field through necessary study," it is nevertheless true that there are nonlawyers whose specialized knowledge and experience may make them as competent as many lawyers in certain areas related to the law. Furthermore, competence of nonlawyers providing services that are included within the definition of the practice of law could be assured, for instance, through experience, education or training standards, certification or licensing, or supervision by a lawyer. In most jurisdictions, the lawyer's continuing competency is supervised through a system of mandatory continuing legal education. Forty-one jurisdictions have such programs with requirements of 10 to 15 hours of education per calendar year. In thirty-eight jurisdictions, the programs also must include ethics education.[14]

Accountability

[16] The existence and utility of methods of accountability for actions taken by anyone providing services that are included within the definition of the practice of law is another key factor for consideration by jurisdictions in determining who should be permitted to provide services that are included within the definition of the practice of law and under what circumstances. Lawyers are made accountable by the rules of professional conduct, a disciplinary system that enforces those rules, court controls such as Rule 11 sanctions and disqualification for conflicts of interest, and established standards of care in civil liability cases.[15]

14. *See* ABA Center for Continuing Legal Education, Summary of MCLE State Requirements, *at* http://www.abanet.org/cle/mcleview.html.

15. *See* RESTATEMENT OF THE LAW THIRD—THE LAW GOVERNING LAWYERS, § 52 (2000).

[17] There are circumstances under which nonlawyers are held accountable pursuant to a state regulatory scheme.[16] In addition, there are federal administrative agencies that permit nonlawyers to represent clients before the agency.[17] These nonlawyers are governed by the agencies' regulations. As part of the process, each jurisdiction should review the scope of permitted services within its definition to determine what level of professional accountability is needed for all who provide the services within the definition. More specifically, jurisdictions should consider whether a law license, another professional license, or a newly formed licensing requirement is needed. They should also determine whether educational or testing requirements, evidence of financial responsibility, continuing education, ethics codes, or other requirements are needed to ensure protection of the public. In some instances, accountability already is assured without the need for any new regulatory system or standards. For instance, there is no regulatory system for paralegals working under the supervision of a lawyer because their accountability is assured through regulation of the lawyer.

Access to Justice

[18] The Task Force believed that defining the practice of law appropriately will improve access to justice. The need for services that are included within the definition of the practice of law is growing and in

---

16. For example, Arizona has recently established (effective April 2003) a Certification and Licensing Program for Legal Document Preparers. *See* Arizona Code of Judicial Administration, Part 7, Chapter 2, § 7-208 (C):

> A. Purpose. The supreme court has inherent regulatory power over all persons providing legal services to the public, regardless of whether they are lawyers or nonlawyers. The court recognizes, however, that the need to protect the public from possible harm caused by nonlawyers providing legal services must be balanced against the public's need for access to legal services. Accordingly, this code section is intended to:
>
> 1. Protect the public through the certification of legal document preparers to ensure conformance to the highest ethical standards and performance of responsibilities in a professional and competent manner, in accordance with all applicable statutes, code sections, and Arizona court rules;
>
> 2. and Result in the effective administration of the Legal Document Preparer Program.

17. For example, the Internal Revenue Service and the Social Security Administration.

many cases does not appear to be met. There are many efforts to meet these needs, some sanctioned by the profession, the courts or the legislature, and others not sanctioned in any way. The growing delivery of services that are included within the definition of the practice of law by nonlawyers presents a dilemma for those who are concerned with both the protection of the public from unqualified persons offering services that are included within the definition of the practice of law and with the need to provide services that are included within the definition of the practice of law to persons otherwise disenfranchised from the legal system.

[19] The Task Force received comments that questioned the existence of evidence of consumer harm from providers of certain services that are included within the definition of the practice of law and cautioned against decreasing access to services provided by nonlawyers without such evidence. Other comments addressed the many benefits provided by nonlawyers supplying services that are included within the definition of the practice of law and the harm to access that would be forthcoming if a broad definition of the practice of law eliminated those nonlawyers as alternative service providers. Thus the Task Force emphasized that the balancing process must be based upon a detailed investigation and determination of facts related to harm and benefit. The evidence should be applied not only to the determination of whether someone should be permitted to provide services that are within the definition of the practice of law, but also to the determination of the extent of regulation, if any, that would be necessary to adequately protect the public in each instance of permitting nonlawyers to deliver services that are included in the definition of the practice of law.

Examples of Service Providers

[20] Several states have identified categories of providers of services that are included within the definition of the practice of law who the jurisdictions have determined are accountable and competent to provide those services in certain circumstances. For example, a person who is licensed in another jurisdiction may be granted authority to engage on a limited basis in transactions, litigation, arbitration, or representation of her employer

business subject to specified requirements that include accountability for the person's actions.[18]

[21] Persons never admitted to practice as lawyers in any jurisdiction also may be permitted to perform services that fall within the definition of practice of law and would be deemed the practice of law if provided by lawyers admitted to practice in the jurisdiction. Supervised law students may provide services that are included within the definition of the practice of law pursuant to supreme court rules.[19] Certified Public Accountants

18. *See* ABA Model Rules of Professional Conduct (2003) Rule 5.5 (2003), providing

> (a) A lawyer admitted in another United States jurisdiction, and not disbarred or suspended from practice in any jurisdiction, may provide legal services on a temporary basis in this jurisdiction that:
>
> > (1) are undertaken in association with a lawyer who is admitted to practice in this jurisdiction and who actively participates in this matter;
> >
> > (2) are in or reasonably related to a pending or potential proceeding before a tribunal in this or another jurisdiction, if the lawyer, or a person the lawyer is assisting, is authorized by law or order too appear in such proceeding or reasonably expects to be so authorized;
> >
> > (3) are in or reasonably related to a pending or potential arbitration, mediation, or other alternative dispute resolution proceeding in this or another jurisdiction, if the services arise out of or are reasonably related to the lawyer's practice in a jurisdiction in which the lawyer is admitted to practice and are not services for which the forum requires pro hac vice admission; or
> >
> > (4) are not within paragraphs (c)(2) or (c)(3) and arise out of or are reasonably related to the lawyer's practice in a jurisdiction in which the lawyer is admitted to practice.
>
> (b) A lawyer admitted in another United States jurisdiction, and not disbarred or suspended from practice in any jurisdiction, may provide legal services in this jurisdiction that:
>
> > (1) are provided to the lawyer's employer or its organizational affiliates and are not services for which the forum requires pro hac vice admission; or
> >
> > (2) are services that the lawyer is authorized to provide by federal law or other law of this jurisdiction.

The laws of two states, Michigan and Virginia, specifically authorize occasional or incidental practice by out-of-state lawyers. Michigan's UPL statute provides that it does not apply to an out-of-state lawyer who is "temporarily in [Michigan] and engaged in a particular matter." The Virginia rules permit an out-of-state lawyer occasionally to provide legal advice or services in Virginia "incidental to representation of a client whom the attorney represents elsewhere." *See* Mich. Comp. Law Ann. § 600.916 and Va. State Bar Rule, Pt. 6, § 1(C).

See also ABA Model Rule for the Licensing of Legal Consultants (*available at* http://www.abanet.org/cpr/mjp/201h.doc) and Model Rule for Temporary Practice by Foreign Lawyers (*available at* http://www.abanet.org/cpr/mjp/201j.doc).

19. *See, e.g.*, Ill. Sup. Ct. R. 711.

may represent others in certain administrative hearings.[20] Paralegal personnel may in most jurisdictions perform functions that would, if done by a lawyer, constitute the practice of law. Authority to do so usually is conditioned upon the person being under the supervision of a member of the bar.[21] Nevertheless, a jurisdiction may prohibit a lawyer who has been disbarred or suspended from performing services permitted of a paralegal even if the disbarred or suspended lawyer were to be supervised by a member of the bar.[22] Customarily, the foregoing matters are appropriately regulated by the courts of a jurisdiction, sometimes within parameters established by the legislature.[23]

[22] The Task Force did not propose a list of specific nonlawyers who should or should not be authorized. It is more constructive for each jurisdiction to undertake its own process, as have Washington, Arizona, the District of Columbia and others, and to carefully study the factors enumerated

---

20. *See, e.g.*, Az. Sup. Ct. R. 31(c)(13).

21. *See, e.g.*, Az. Sup. Ct. R. 31(c) (Regulation of the Practice of Law)

> (c) Exceptions. Notwithstanding the provisions of section (b):
>
> * * *
>
> 15. Nothing in this rule shall affect the ability of nonlawyer assistants to act under the supervision of a lawyer in compliance with Rule 5.3 of the rules of professional conduct.

See also, Washington Court Rules—Part I—Rules of General Application—General Rules— GR 24 (Definition of the Practice of Law)

> * * *
>
> (c) Nonlawyer Assistants: Nothing in this rule shall affect the ability of nonlawyer assistants to act under the supervision of a lawyer in compliance with Rule 5.3 of the Rules of Professional Conduct.

22. *See, e.g.*, Ill. Sup. Ct. R. 764(b) (a suspended or disbarred lawyer may not "maintain a presence or occupy an office" where a law practice is being conducted); Wis. Sup. Ct. R. 22.26 (a suspended or disbarred lawyer may not engage in any "law work activity customarily done by law students, law clerks or other paralegal personnel, except . . . in law-related work for a commercial employer not itself engaged in the practice of law.").

23. *See* Recommendation 201A, adopted by the ABA House of Delegates in August 2002: "RESOLVED, that the American Bar Association affirms its support for the principle of state judicial regulation of the practice of law." (The full Report is available at http://www.abanet.org/cpr/mjp/201a.doc).

in the third resolution in light of its own unique circumstances.[24] That said, it would still be useful for jurisdictions to consider in their studies the examples of authorized providers that the Task Force gathered from around the country.[25]

IMPLEMENTATION

[23] The Task Force recommended a set of principles to be used in the implementation of a procedural framework for defining the practice of law and the determination of who may provide services that are included within the definition under certain conditions. These principles will aid the states in the process of establishing the framework and ultimately in the difficult process of weighing the factors of minimum qualifications, competence and accountability.

(a) Comprehensive studies of harm and potential harm should be conducted concerning the provision of services that are included within the definition of the practice of law by lawyers and nonlawyers and weighed

24. The August 1995 Report of the ABA Commission on Nonlawyer Practice stated that:

> [T]he most important conclusion of the Commission is that each state should conduct its own careful analytical examination, under the leadership of its supreme court, to determine whether and how to regulate the varied forms of nonlawyer activity that exist or are emerging in its jurisdiction.
>
> . . . .
>
> The Commission recommends a specific analytical approach for use by the state in determining what level of regulation, if any, is appropriate. The approach will help in assessing whether a particular activity should be unregulated, regulated or prohibited. Three broad criteria are suggested:
>
> 1. Does the nonlawyer activity pose a serious risk to the consumer's life, health, safety or economic well-being?
>
> 2. Do potential consumers of law-related nonlawyer services have the knowledge needed to properly evaluate the qualifications of nonlawyers offering the services?
>
> 3. Do the actual benefits of regulation likely to accrue to the public outweigh any likely negative consequences of regulation?
>
> . . . .
>
> At the root of this balancing of interests lies a difficult question, which a state will have to answer based on its particular culture and values. What should be the level of trade off, if any, between a consumer's interest in having at least some assistance from a nonlawyer and the increased risk of harm from the possibly less qualified assistance of a nonlawyer?

NONLAWYER ACTIVITY IN LAW-RELATED SITUATIONS at 136, 137.

25. *See* http://www.abanet.org/cpr/model-def/model_def_statutes.pdf for exceptions listed among the definitions of the practice of law.

against potential benefits of allowing additional service providers. For example, Arizona spent over a year studying complaints filed at the bar against unlicensed providers in determining which areas needed continued or additional regulation and which areas might allow new services by nonlawyers.

(b) In the initial process of analyzing evidence and in subsequent reviews of harm and benefit there should be a diverse, impartial cross section of representation from the legal profession, other relevant professions and the public as a whole. A definition of the practice of law directly affects not only lawyers, but also consumers of services that are included within the definition of the practice of law and nonlawyer providers.

(c) There should be a process in each jurisdiction for the continual review of both the definition of the practice of law and who may provide services that are included within the definition under certain circumstances to take into account changing market factors and other additional evidence, with an eye to the future. Examples of such processes already in place include the hearing process used by the Florida Supreme Court to determine the appropriate parameters of who may provide services within the definition of the practice of law based upon a weighing of potential harm versus possible benefits to the public.[26] Likewise, the establishment in Washington of the Washington Practice of Law Board allows a similar review.[27] A board such as Washington's should include representatives from many constituent bodies.

(d) Each review should give careful consideration to evidence of accountability and competence of other regulated professionals and of lawyers licensed in other jurisdictions, examining whether there already exist sufficient controls to allow them to provide services that are included

26. *See* Rules Regulating the Florida Bar Rule § 10-9.1 (Procedures for Issuance of Advisory Opinions on the Unlicensed Practice of Law).

27. *See* http://www.abanet.org/cpr/model-def/atj_gr24.pdf for the rules of the Washington Practice of Law Board. Washington's Practice of Law Board is charged with issuing advisory opinions on the practice of law, investigating complaints regarding unauthorized practice and making recommendations to the Supreme Court regarding any changes to the definition as well as any areas of practice that might be appropriate for limited licensing of nonlawyers. (For example, Washington has had a limited licensing of nonlawyers to practice certain defined aspects of the practice of law in real property closings since 1983.)

within the definition of the practice of law in the jurisdiction reviewing their possible entry.[28]

[24] Implementation requires adequate resources, funding and periodic review, as does enforcement. Far fewer resources are devoted nationally to enforcement of remedies and sanctions against nonlawyers than against lawyers. If additional service providers are authorized under certain conditions, then those conditions must be enforced.

Conclusion

[25] Many jurisdictions have left the determination as to what constitutes the practice of law to a case-by-case analysis. As a result, there are an increasing number of situations where nonlawyers, or lawyers licensed in a different jurisdiction, are providing services that are difficult to categorize under current state authority as being, or not being, the delivery of services that are included within the definition of the practice of law. The adoption of a definition of the practice of law is a necessary step in protecting the public from unqualified service providers and in eliminating qualified providers' uncertainty about the propriety of their conduct in any particular jurisdiction.

[26] The Task Force believed that each jurisdiction's definition should include the basic premise that the practice of law is the application of legal principles and judgment to the circumstances or objectives of another person or entity. This basic premise is not a model for a definition, but rather a part of a framework.

[27] Upon adding elements to the basic premise, each jurisdiction should then use a balancing process to determine who may provide services that are included within the jurisdiction's definition of the practice of law and under what circumstances, based upon the potential harm and benefit to the public. The determination should include consideration of

28. A regulatory approach for nonlawyer activity may be needed if the activity presents a serious risk of harm, if consumers cannot protect themselves against that risk because they will find it difficult or impossible to evaluate the nonlawyer service provider's qualifications, or if the likely benefits of regulation outweigh the likely negative consequences of regulation. The type of regulation chosen will depend upon the predicted costs and effectiveness (of different regulatory options) in reducing the predicted harm while avoiding counterbalancing negative consequences. The activity should be prohibited if no regulatory approach will effectively accomplish an appropriate level of public protection.

minimum qualifications, competence and accountability. The results may differ from jurisdiction to jurisdiction.

[28] In creating the definition, the jurisdiction must consider regulatory concerns. There must be sufficient resources to maintain any additional regulatory procedures resulting from a change in the jurisdiction's current approach. In the discharge of its fundamental role to regulate the practice of law, the judicial branch of government should participate in defining the practice of law and in establishing a regulatory structure that promotes access to justice, accountability, and client protection. Since protection of the public is a paramount goal of the legal profession and of the justice system it serves, the regulatory process should enforce accountability by all who provide services within the definition of the practice of law.

ABA MODEL COURT RULE ON INSURANCE DISCLOSURE

Adopted by the American Bar Association House of Delegates on August 10, 2004.

American Bar Association
Standing Committee on Client Protection
2003–2004

Robert D. Welden, *Chair*
Seattle, Washington

Melissa DeLacerda
Stillwater, Oklahoma

A. Root Edmonson
Raleigh, North Carolina

Gwendolyn Hodge
Little Rock, Arkansas

Lori S. Holcomb
Tallahassee, Florida

Henry A. Kelly
Albuquerque, New Mexico

Lynda C. Shely
Scottsdale, Arizona

Alice E. Richmond, *Liaison*
ABA Board of Governors
Boston, Massachusetts

Carole R. Richelieu, *Liaison*
National Client Protection Organization
Honolulu, Hawaii

G. Fred Ours, *Liaison*
National Organization of Bar Counsel
Baton Rouge, Louisiana

Center for Professional Responsibility

Director
Jeanne P. Gray

Client Protection Counsel
John A. Holtaway

MODEL COURT RULE ON INSURANCE DISCLOSURE

PREFACE

The ABA *Model Court Rule on Insurance Disclosure* requires lawyers to disclose on their annual registration statements whether they maintain professional liability insurance. The Model Court Rule excludes from the Rule's reporting requirement those lawyers who are not engaged in the active practice of law and those who are engaged in the practice of law as full-time government lawyers or as counsel employed by an organizational client and do not represent clients outside that capacity. The Model Court Rule places an affirmative duty upon lawyers to notify the highest court whenever the insurance policy covering the lawyer's conduct lapses or is terminated. This ensures that the information reported to the highest court is accurate during the entire reporting period. Lawyers who do not comply with the Model Court Rule are not unauthorized to practice law until they comply.

The purpose of the Model Court Rule is to provide a potential client with access to relevant information related to a lawyer's representation in order to make an informed decision about whether to hire a particular lawyer. The Model Court Rule is a balanced standard that allows potential clients to obtain relevant information about a lawyer if they initiate an inquiry, while placing a modest annual reporting requirement on lawyers. The information submitted by lawyers will be made available by such means as designated by the highest court in the jurisdiction.

A. Each lawyer admitted to the active practice of law shall certify to the [highest court of the jurisdiction] on or before [December 31 of each year]: 1) whether the lawyer is engaged in the private practice of law; 2) if engaged in the private practice of law, whether the lawyer is currently covered by professional liability insurance; 3) whether the lawyer intends to maintain insurance during the period of time the lawyer is engaged in the private practice of law; and 4) whether the lawyer is exempt from the provisions of this Rule because the lawyer is engaged in the practice of law as a full-time government lawyer or is counsel employed by an organizational client and does not represent clients outside that capacity. Each lawyer admitted to the active

practice of law in this jurisdiction who reports being covered by professional liability insurance shall notify [the highest court in the jurisdiction] in writing within 30 days if the insurance policy providing coverage lapses, is no longer in effect or terminates for any reason.

B. **The foregoing shall be certified by each lawyer admitted to the active practice of law in this jurisdiction in such form as may be prescribed by the [highest court of the jurisdiction]. The information submitted pursuant to this Rule will be made available to the public by such means as may be designated by the [highest court of the jurisdiction].**

C. **Any lawyer admitted to the active practice of law who fails to comply with this Rule in a timely fashion, as defined by the [highest court in the jurisdiction], may be suspended from the practice of law until such time as the lawyer complies. Supplying false information in response to this Rule shall subject the lawyer to appropriate disciplinary action.**

ABA MODEL COURT RULE ON PROVISION OF LEGAL SERVICES FOLLOWING DETERMINATION OF MAJOR DISASTER

Adopted by the American Bar Association House of Delegates on February 12, 2007.

American Bar Association
Standing Committee on Client Protection
2006–2007

Janet Green Marbley, *Chair*
Columbus, Ohio

Carla J. Freudenburg
Washington, D.C.

Justice Randy Holland
Wilmington, Delaware

Victoria Kremski
Lansing, Michigan

Timothy O'Sullivan
Albany, New York

Carole R. Richelieu
Honolulu, Hawaii

Robert D. Welden
Seattle, Washington

Richard T. Cassidy, *Liaison*
ABA Board of Governors
Burlington, Vermont

A. Root Edmonson, *Liaison*
National Client Protection Organization
Raleigh, North Carolina

Donald R. Lundberg, *Liaison*
National Organization of Bar Counsel
Indianapolis, Indiana

Center for Professional Responsibility

Director
Jeanne P. Gray

Client Protection Counsel
John A. Holtaway

MODEL COURT RULE ON PROVISION OF LEGAL SERVICES FOLLOWING DETERMINATION OF MAJOR DISASTER

PREFACE

In the summer of 2005, Alabama, Louisiana and Mississippi were devastated by Hurricanes Katrina and Rita. The physical damage done in those jurisdictions was catastrophic but the storms also damaged and crippled their legal systems. The *Model Court Rule on Provision of Legal Services Following Determination of Major Disaster* provides that, after the highest court in an affected jurisdiction, or in another jurisdiction to which displaced persons temporarily relocate, determines that an emergency exists that affects the state's justice system and the provision of legal services, the court may allow: (1) out-of-state lawyers to provide *pro bono* legal services to the citizens of the affected state within certain constraints described in the model rule; and (2) lawyers from an affected state can provide legal services in an unaffected state on a temporary basis if these services are reasonably related to the lawyer's practice in the affected jurisdiction. The provision of temporary *pro bono* legal services under the Model Court Rule shall be assigned and supervised through an established not-for-profit bar association, *pro bono* program or legal services program or through such organization specifically designated by the highest court. The Model Court Rule requires out-of-state lawyers to file a registration statement with the Clerk of the Court in a form prescribed by the Court. Under paragraph (b) of the Model Court Rule, an *emeritus* lawyer from another United States jurisdiction may provide *pro bono* legal services on a temporary basis in an affected jurisdiction.

The Model Court Rule incorporates the fundamental and well-settled Association policy that regulation of the legal profession vests with the judicial branch of government.

Provision of Legal Services Following Determination of Major Disaster

A. *Determination of existence of major disaster.* Solely for purposes of this Rule, this Court shall determine when an emergency affecting the justice system, as a result of a natural or other major disaster has occurred in:

(1) this jurisdiction and whether the emergency caused by the major disaster affects the entirety or only a part of this jurisdiction, or

(2) another jurisdiction but only after such a determination and its geographical scope have been made by the highest court of that jurisdiction. The authority to engage in the temporary practice of law in this jurisdiction pursuant to paragraph (c) shall extend only to lawyers who principally practice in the area of such other jurisdiction determined to have suffered a major disaster causing an emergency affecting the justice system and the provision of legal services.

B. *Temporary practice in this jurisdiction following major disaster.* Following the determination of an emergency affecting the justice system in this jurisdiction pursuant to paragraph (a) of this Rule, or a determination that persons displaced by a major disaster in another jurisdiction and residing in this jurisdiction are in need of pro bono services and the assistance of lawyers from outside of this jurisdiction is required to help provide such assistance, a lawyer authorized to practice law in another United States jurisdiction, and not disbarred, suspended from practice or otherwise restricted from practice in any jurisdiction, may provide legal services in this jurisdiction on a temporary basis. Such legal services must be provided on a *pro bono* basis without compensation, expectation of compensation or other direct or indirect pecuniary gain to the lawyer. Such legal services shall be assigned and supervised through an established not-for-profit bar association, *pro bono* program or legal services program or through such organization(s) specifically designated by this Court.

C. *Temporary practice in this jurisdiction following major disaster in another jurisdiction.* Following the determination of a major disaster in another United States jurisdiction, a lawyer who is authorized to practice law and who principally practices in that affected jurisdiction, and who is not disbarred, suspended from practice or otherwise restricted from practice in any jurisdiction, may provide legal services in this jurisdiction on a temporary basis. Those legal services must arise out of and be reasonably related to that lawyer's practice of law in the jurisdiction, or area of such other jurisdiction, where the major disaster occurred.

D. *Duration of authority for temporary practice.* The authority to practice law in this jurisdiction granted by paragraph (b) of this Rule shall end when this Court determines that the conditions caused by the major disaster in this jurisdiction have ended except that a lawyer then representing clients in this jurisdiction pursuant to paragraph (b) is authorized to continue the provision of legal services for such time as is reasonably necessary to complete the representation, but the lawyer shall not thereafter accept new clients. The authority to practice law in this jurisdiction granted by paragraph (c) of this Rule shall end [60] days after this Court declares that the conditions caused by the major disaster in the affected jurisdiction have ended.

E. *Court appearances.* The authority granted by this Rule does not include appearances in court except:
   (1) pursuant to that court's *pro hac vice* admission rule and, if such authority is granted, any fees for such admission shall be waived; or
   (2) if this Court, in any determination made under paragraph (a), grants blanket permission to appear in all or designated courts of this jurisdiction to lawyers providing legal services pursuant to paragraph (b). If such an authorization is included, any *pro hac vice* admission fees shall be waived.

F. *Disciplinary authority and registration requirement.* Lawyers providing legal services in this jurisdiction pursuant to paragraphs (b) or (c) are subject to this Court's disciplinary authority and the *Rules of Professional Conduct* of this jurisdiction as provided in Rule 8.5 of the *Rules of Professional* Conduct. Lawyers providing legal services in this jurisdiction under paragraphs (b) or (c) shall, within 30 days from the commencement of the provision of legal services, file a registration statement with

the Clerk of this Court. The registration statement shall be in a form prescribed by this Court. Any lawyer who provides legal services pursuant to this Rule shall not be considered to be engaged in the unlawful practice of law in this jurisdiction.

G. *Notification to clients.* **Lawyers authorized to practice law in another United States jurisdiction who provide legal services pursuant to this Rule shall inform clients in this jurisdiction of the jurisdiction in which they are authorized to practice law, any limits of that authorization, and that they are not authorized to practice law in this jurisdiction except as permitted by this Rule. They shall not state or imply to any person that they are otherwise authorized to practice law in this jurisdiction.**

Comment

[1] A major disaster in this or another jurisdiction may cause an emergency affecting the justice system with respect to the provision of legal services for a sustained period of time interfering with the ability of lawyers admitted and practicing in the affected jurisdiction to continue to represent clients until the disaster has ended. When this happens, lawyers from the affected jurisdiction may need to provide legal services to their clients, on a temporary basis, from an office outside their home jurisdiction. In addition, lawyers in an unaffected jurisdiction may be willing to serve residents of the affected jurisdiction who have unmet legal needs as a result of the disaster or, though independent of the disaster, whose legal needs temporarily are unmet because of disruption to the practices of local lawyers. Lawyers from unaffected jurisdictions may offer to provide these legal services either by traveling to the affected jurisdiction or from their own offices or both, provided the legal services are provided on a *pro bono* basis through an authorized not-for-profit entity or such other organization(s) specifically designated by this Court. A major disaster includes, for example, a hurricane, earthquake, flood, wildfire, tornado, public health emergency or an event caused by terrorists or acts of war.

[2] Under paragraph (a)(1), this Court shall determine whether a major disaster causing an emergency affecting the justice system has occurred in this jurisdiction, or in a part of this jurisdiction, for purposes of triggering paragraph (b) of this Rule. This Court may, for example, determine that the entirety of this jurisdiction has suffered a disruption in the provision of legal services or that only certain areas have suffered such an

event. The authority granted by paragraph (b) shall extend only to lawyers authorized to practice law and not disbarred, suspended from practice or otherwise restricted from practice in any other manner in any other jurisdiction.

[3] Paragraph (b) permits lawyers authorized to practice law in an unaffected jurisdiction, and not disbarred, suspended from practice or otherwise restricted from practicing law in any other manner in any other jurisdiction, to provide pro bono legal services to residents of the affected jurisdiction following determination of an emergency caused by a major disaster; notwithstanding that they are not otherwise authorized to practice law in the affected jurisdiction. Other restrictions on a lawyer's license to practice law that would prohibit that lawyer from providing legal services pursuant to this Rule include, but are not limited to, probation, inactive status, disability inactive status or a non-disciplinary administrative suspension for failure to complete continuing legal education or other requirements. Lawyers on probation may be subject to monitoring and specific limitations on their practices. Lawyers on inactive status, despite being characterized in many jurisdictions as being "in good standing," and lawyers on disability inactive status are not permitted to practice law. Public protection warrants exclusion of these lawyers from the authority to provide legal services as defined in this Rule. Lawyers permitted to provide legal services pursuant to this Rule must do so without fee or other compensation, or expectation thereof. Their service must be provided through an established not-for-profit organization that is authorized to provide legal services either in its own name or that provides representation of clients through employed or cooperating lawyers. Alternatively, this court may instead designate other specific organization(s) through which these legal services may be rendered. Under paragraph (b), an *emeritus* lawyer from another United State jurisdiction may provide *pro bono* legal services on a temporary basis in this jurisdiction provided that the *emeritus* lawyer is authorized to provide *pro bono* legal services in that jurisdiction pursuant to that jurisdiction's *emeritus* or *pro bono* practice rule. Lawyers may also be authorized to provide legal services in this jurisdiction on a temporary basis under Rule 5.5(c) of the *Rules of Professional Conduct*.

[4] Lawyers authorized to practice law in another jurisdiction, who principally practice in the area of such other jurisdiction determined by this Court to have suffered a major disaster, and whose practices are disrupted by a major disaster there, and who are not disbarred, suspended from

practice or otherwise restricted from practicing law in any other manner in any other jurisdiction, are authorized under paragraph (c) to provide legal services on a temporary basis in this jurisdiction. Those legal services must arise out of and be reasonably related to the lawyer's practice of law in the affected jurisdiction. For purposes of this Rule, the determination of a major disaster in another jurisdiction should first be made by the highest court of appellate jurisdiction in that jurisdiction. For the meaning of "arise out of and reasonably related to," see Rule 5.5 Comment [14], *Rules of Professional Conduct*.

[5] Emergency conditions created by major disasters end, and when they do, the authority created by paragraphs (b) and (c) also ends with appropriate notice to enable lawyers to plan and to complete pending legal matters. Under paragraph (d), this Court determines when those conditions end only for purposes of this Rule. The authority granted under paragraph (b) shall end upon such determination except that lawyers assisting residents of this jurisdiction under paragraph (b) may continue to do so for such longer period as is reasonably necessary to complete the representation. The authority created by paragraph (c) will end [60] days after this Court makes such a determination with regard to an affected jurisdiction.

[6] Paragraphs (b) and (c) do not authorize lawyers to appear in the courts of this jurisdiction. Court appearances are subject to the *pro hac vice* admission rules of the particular court. This Court may, in a determination made under paragraph (e)(2), include authorization for lawyers who provide legal services in this jurisdiction under paragraph (b) to appear in all or designated courts of this jurisdiction without need for such *pro hac vice* admission. If such an authorization is included, any *pro hac vice* admission fees shall be waived. A lawyer who has appeared in the courts of this jurisdiction pursuant to paragraph (e) may continue to appear in any such matter notwithstanding a declaration under paragraph (d) that the conditions created by major disaster have ended. Furthermore, withdrawal from a court appearance is subject to Rule 1.16 of the *Rules of Professional Conduct*.

[7] Authorization to practice law as a foreign legal consultant or in-house counsel in a United States jurisdiction offers lawyers a limited scope of permitted practice and may therefore restrict that person's ability to provide legal services under this Rule.

[8] The ABA National Lawyer Regulatory Data Bank is available to help determine whether any lawyer seeking to practice in this jurisdiction pursuant to paragraphs (b) or (c) of this Rule is disbarred, suspended from practice or otherwise subject to a public disciplinary sanction that would restrict the lawyer's ability to practice law in any other jurisdiction.

Subject Guide to the Compendium of Client Protection Rules

D

W